Gender
&
Desire

NUMBER SIX:
Carolyn and Ernest Fay Series
in Analytical Psychology
David H. Rosen, General Editor

Polly Young-Eisendrath

Gender & Desire

Uncursing Pandora

Foreword by
David H. Rosen

Texas A&M University Press
College Station

The paper used in this book meets the minimum requirements
of the American National Standard for Permanence
of Paper for Printed Library Materials, Z39.48–1984.
Binding materials have been chosen for durability.

Library of Congress Cataloging-in-Publication Data

Young-Eisendrath, Polly, 1947–
    Gender and desire : uncursing Pandora / Polly Young-Eisendrath ;
foreword by David H. Rosen.
        p.   cm. — (Carolyn and Ernest Fay series in analytical psychology ;
no. 6)
    Includes bibliographical references and index.
    ISBN 0–89096–746–6 (cloth : alk. paper)
    1. Sexism.   2. Gender.   3. Desire.   4. Psychoanalysis and feminism.
5. Jungian psychology.   6. Feminist psychology.   I. Title.   II. Series.
BF175.5.S52Y68   1997   96–39207
155.3—dc21   CIP

Number Six
CAROLYN AND ERNEST FAY SERIES
IN ANALYTICAL PSYCHOLOGY
David H. Rosen, General Editor

The Carolyn and Ernest Fay edited book series, based initially on the annual Fay Lecture Series in Analytical Psychology, was established to further the ideas of C. G. Jung among students, faculty, therapists, and other citizens and to enhance scholarly activities related to analytical psychology. The Book Series and Lecture Series address topics of importance to the individual and to society. Both series were generously endowed by Carolyn Grant Fay, the founding president of the C. G. Jung Educational Center in Houston, Texas. The series are in part a memorial to her late husband, Ernest Bel Fay. Carolyn Fay has planted a Jungian tree carrying both her name and that of her late husband, which will bear fruitful ideas and stimulate creative works from this time forward. Texas A&M University and all those who come in contact with the growing Fay Jungian tree are extremely grateful to Carolyn Grant Fay for what she has done. The holder of the Frank N. McMillan, Jr. Professorship in Analytical Psychology at Texas A&M functions as the general editor of the Fay Book Series.

Contents

Foreword

*It is fatal to be a man or woman pure and simple; one must be
woman-manly or man-womanly . . . And fatal is no figure of speech;
for anything written with a conscious bias is doomed to death. It
ceases to be fertilized . . . Some collaboration has to take place in the
mind between the woman and the man before the action of creation
can be accomplished. Some marriage of opposites has to be consum-
mated.*[1]

—Virginia Woolf

Dr. Polly Young-Eisendrath embraces Virginia Woolf's prescrip-
tion and this book represents an act of creation that will endure.
Young-Eisendrath is a true scholar: a learned person and an original thinker. She's also brave, challenging us to think in new ways.
In the past, Young-Eisendrath has confronted sexism in certain aspects of analytical psychology.[2] In this work she shows how and
why this sexism arises and offers a postmodern (post-Jungian) perspective that both allows her to embrace analytical psychology
and to help us grow through transformative understanding. In addition, she is a great teacher who through word (speaking and writing) and deed (embodying her topic) has as her goal to change the
way you think about things.

She changed the minds of many of my students, among whom

was a young man in the Corps of Cadets. The Corps, with two thousand members, is a visible symbol of the past at Texas A&M University (TAMU), a previously all male uniformed military college. Today TAMU is integrated in every way, and half of the forty-five thousand student population is female. My student was skeptical about attending lectures given by an "ardent feminist." However, he was motivated by the possibility of raising his grade. In evaluating Young-Eisendrath's Fay Lecture Series in a review essay, he wrote that the ideas that she presented had changed his views about women and men forever. Courageously he admitted that his opposition to feminism, in particular, had been based on prejudiced ideas that he had incorporated from the culture at large. His transformation from an unexamined sexism to an active, conscious feminism was especially notable because of the military nature of his academic experience. This example illustrates how Dr. Young-Eisendrath effectively communicates her ideas, facilitating change even in the most resistant individuals.

This book resulted from Dr. Young-Eisendrath's Fay Lectures on "Gender, Myth, and Desire." The basic myth she explores is now named in the book's subtitle *Gender and Desire: Uncursing Pandora*. In myth, a tale larger than life, there is an articulation of something we ardently desire. Pandora (the first woman of ancient patriarchal Greek mythology), like the Biblical Eve, is a beautiful but empty temptress. In our culture, there is a passionate longing for the patriarchal prototype of the object of desire who promises pleasure and power. Women identify with her and men want to possess her. But her power is deceptive and misleading as it is based on illusion. Nevertheless, like the yin of the Taoist yin/yang symbol, this dark symbol contains light. After Pandora opens the earthenware jar and all the evils are released into the world, hope remains in the form of a bird (a symbol of the spirit world). Hope connects us to what Young-Eisendrath calls the fundamental transcendent coherence of our universe, referred to by Jung as the

Self—a sacred unifying principle. Making sense of Pandora, we come to a new vision of women and men.

Young-Eisendrath focuses in detail on the Pandora myth which she deconstructs. In the process, which involves us by *participation mystique*, it becomes clear that we must uncurse and liberate Pandora and help transform her into a healthy woman of our time. The issue of gender becomes reality based with the human experience of the contrasexual aspect of our own psyches. For men, this means relating to and with the contrasexual "feminine" or inner woman in a different way, expressed in their relationships with women. For women, it means actualizing the contrasexual "masculine" or inner man and becoming whole, that is, becoming their own subjects of desire.

In this small volume Dr. Young-Eisendrath outlines a way, which if followed will lead to more harmonious inner and outer relationships. It will also hopefully help to reverse the outer hatred of the opposite sex and the epidemic of divorce that plagues our culture.

At the outset in chapter one, "The Problem of Realism in Analytical Psychology," Dr. Young-Eisendrath uses an analogy of baseball umpires to illustrate three world views: premodern, modern, and postmodern. The premodern umpire is an empiricist whose reality is based on observation: "I calls 'em as I sees 'em." The modern umpire is a realist whose truth is based on fact: "I calls 'em as they are." Finally, the postmodern umpire is a relativist who knows that all facts and truths are rooted in subjective understanding: "They ain't nothin' 'til I calls 'em!" I like the umpire analogy, the sense of fairness it represents, and that each umpire has a uniquely valuable perspective. The three views seem to reflect our past, present, and future, and are all vital to an integrated view of reality. However, it is clear that the postmodern view brings reality home and makes it part of our human experience: we are forced to own up to our role in shaping reality. A lived postmodern philosophy is essential for change to occur.

Dr. Young-Eisendrath rightly critiques analytical psychology for freezing and reifying some concepts such as anima and animus. I believe that Jung himself would have criticized a dogmatic approach; after all, he wrote, "I criticize Freudian psychology for a certain narrowness and bias, and the Freudians for a certain rigid, sectarian spirit of intolerance and fanaticism. I proclaim no cut-and-dried doctrine and I abhor 'blind adherents.'"[3] My hunch is that Jung would have supported Young-Eisendrath's emphasis on constructivism and hermeneutics. While Jung discovered meaning through ideas, he also did this through a process of deconstruction, hermeneutics, and constructivism. For example, as early as Jung's break with Freud, Jung was deconstructing Freud's patriarchal view of women. Jung's innovative ideas of anima and animus (which Young-Eisendrath carefully deconstructs) were also deconstructed and reconstructed through a hermeneutical process by Jung himself when he actualized "the inner marriage" in his later years.[4]

In her second chapter on "Gender, Contrasexuality, and Self," Young-Eisendrath defines sex as a biological constraint that is inflexible and gender as a social construct which is flexible and dependent on context. There are only two gender clubs for humans and this division leads to some important psychological developments. Dr. Young-Eisendrath accurately states that most psychological theories, including Jung's, were developed by men and were (and are) patriarchal or androcentric. Her post-Jungian perspective, one of shared power and gender equality, is similar to other post-Jungian theorists such as Verena Kast, June Singer, and Demaris Wehr who all see "androgyny" and its association with individuation and mental health as a goal for women and men to attain.[5]

Dr. Young-Eisendrath introduces the concept of the "other," "strange gender," or "dream lover" (the contrasexual aspect of the psyche) which we initially project onto the opposite sex. Young-Eisendrath underscores that the androcentric socio-cultural milieu we live in is grossly unfair to women. For example, it's fine for girls to be tom boys but it's not okay for boys to be tom girls! Because of the cultural emphasis on possessing objects, jealously flourishes in our society. Envy (an even more primitive emotion): a desire to destroy, also thrives in our culture. Falling in love represents the flip side of envy, i.e. the idealization of women, which is a hollow patriarchal Pandora scenario. Love and intimacy ought to begin at home with the love of the contrasexual aspect of oneself, that is, the inner love of the other within. This "inner marriage" allows us to love another person of the opposite sex with authenticity, equality, and mutuality.

Dr. Young-Eisendrath's third chapter "Pandora and the Object of Desire" focuses on women as objects of desire. In other words, according to the patriarchy, women are there to please and fulfill men. The living myth of Pandora says to women: be beautiful and you'll have power. But this power is also labeled as manipulative, empty, and negative. In the myth, Pandora has deceit in place of heart. Like in the lower levels of Buddhist hell, contemporary Pandora has an insatiable desire and she is searching for satisfaction. Similarly to the Buddhist hungry ghost, she is driven by rage and emptiness. However, Pandora's curiosity contains the seed of her (and our) salvation. By opening the jar that the patriarch said not to open, she let's out all the evils (disease, death, etc.), but hope remains. So there is hope that a transformation can and will take place.

The patriarchal emphasis on outer beauty has led so many women to sacrifice their bodies and 'true selves.' Mary Pipher's superb book, *Reviving Ophelia*, documents the tragic effects of sexism and what she calls "lookism" on adolescent girls.[6] The eating disorders (anorexia nervosa, bulimia, excessive thinness, and overeating) represent some of the negative fallout from living the Pandora myth. Rape and other forms of violence toward women are disastrous results of this patriarchal curse. In men these anti-female urges translate into suicidal rages against their own souls and inner contrasexuality. As a culture, we must wake up to the effects of this living myth and transform its curse. Feminism and postmodernism demand that we view each other—men and women—as equals and with reverence.

Dr. Young-Eisendrath's last chapter on "Subject of Desire," focuses on uncursing Pandora. She must find her lost heart and soul. Pandora must love her inner "other" or "strange gender." Subsequently, each woman needs to actualize her full potential. We are all in need of a fundamental shift: We must get beyond the dominance myth of the patriarchy which necessitates uncursing and liberating of Pandora. This is what feminism was (and is) about: The human experience of each woman becoming her own person. Men must understand that uncursing Pandora liberates not only women but also themselves.

Dr. Young-Eisendrath's illuminating and timely book promises hope and provides the needed postmodern remedy called for by Demaris Wehr:

> The next step for Jungians is to step back and allow the "feminine" to arise out of women's experience, not imposing, on this term, or on women, Jung's ambivalence or the culture- and gender-based limitations of his perspective.[7]

David H. Rosen
College Station, Texas

Preface

When I was invited to give the Fay Lectures at Texas A&M University, I wondered whether I would be able to convey in lecture form, and then in writing, the complexity of the psychological nature of gender and desire as I have encountered them in my practice and my life. What seems most significant psychologically about gender is the *division* of the human community into two mutually exclusive groups. The issue of gender as division has not been fully explored, although such exploration has begun among our European colleagues in psychoanalysis and feminism, particularly the followers of French psychiatrist Jacques Lacan.

This division of the human community into two mutually exclusive groups leads to a division of the human psyche into a self and a particular type of other—the other of the opposite sex. In the history of psychoanalysis, this idea is first expressed in Jung's theory of a "contrasexual" personality, a personality (less conscious than our own gendered self) that develops alongside of what is considered to be self. The topic of contrasexuality is complex enough that many people have misunderstood it or misused it to type and stereotype people.

Even today, among contemporary psychologists and psychoanalysts, the terrain of gender is crisscrossed by contradictory and provocative pathways. Exploring it was still more confusing in earlier centuries, when women, by and large, did not speak for themselves, but primarily were stereotyped and/or depicted as idealized or devalued symbols.

In my own studies of philosophy and feminism, I have toiled to clear a path through this difficult terrain—a path that has led me and others to new clarity about identity, gender, and desire. I wanted to present all this to the audience at Texas A&M University and then make sense of it in a written text.

In the course of an initial attempt to pull together my thoughts, I remembered how useful the myth of Pandora had been in my previous unpublished explorations of gender and desire. Pandora, the first woman (i.e., mortal, not goddess) in Greek mythology, symbolizes much of what it means to be known as a woman in patriarchal society—and, by extension, what it is to be known as a man. Pandora is created by Zeus as a punishment to men (the only humans living at the time) for having stolen fire from the gods. She is to be a curse to men, an evil that they will hold close to their hearts, that is comparable to the boon of fire. At the end of the twentieth century, in the wake of what has been the most successful wave of feminism ever to be recorded, Pandora's curse—a beauty that holds power over men—is still upon us. The myth of a manipulative, deceitful, "desire-awakening maiden"—Pandora's story—pervades our culture, as girls and women strive to be the objects of desire, while all of us (both women and men) treat female appearance as a commodity to be bought and sold. Men are caught up in Pandora's story when they believe that women use their appearance to exert power over men.

In working to liberate us all from the curse of Pandora, I discovered a theory of desire: desire contains within it a primordial absence, a sense that something is missing. Desire becomes desire only when something is lacking. Desire always will contain within it this seed of absence. Consequently, we can never wholly satisfy our desires. If we identify with desire (especially if we identify with it unconsciously and want to be the *object* of desire), then we are always restless, driven, off-center. Pandora does not know what she desires; she is aware only of a need to be seen and known in a particular way. Pandora would rather be popular than smart—not because she understands the difference, but rather because she lacks a sense of her own self, a clear identity. Some men also have this problem, but as the story of Pandora shows us, a major problem lies within the category of Woman, in what we unconsciously may assume is true about being female.

As I pursued this problem of desire—who is the subject and who is the object?—I found that two contexts, in addition to Jung's psychology of contrasexuality, were helpful. One was affirmative postmodernism—the theories of hermeneutics and constructivism. Hermeneutics is the theory of interpretation or knowledge, which holds that human interpretations underlie all that we think and do, no matter how objective and scientific or spiritual and intuitive we try to be. The constraints of being human limit our knowledge of truth and guarantee that what we take to be truth always will change. Constructivism is the perspective that the phenomenal world, the world of our experience of time-space-causality, is construed or constructed from the active engagement of human beings with an environment in flux. Because universally we are embodied in a particular form (including capacities for language, thought, emotion), we humans share a world. What we take to be "reality out there" is the product of our own perceptions, engaged with a world that we never can know directly. These two theories—hermeneutics and constructivism—have helped me describe a postmodern analytical psychology of gender and desire.

In addition to affirmative postmodernism, I drew upon Buddhism as a means to develop a theory of Self that is not essentialist, a theory of the archetype of individual subjectivity in a framework of increasing coherence over a lifespan. Buddhism, like postmodernism, is a critique of metaphysics without being a new metaphysics. Buddhism, like postmodernism, emphasizes the gains connected to seeing our limits and our impermanence. Buddhism adds the value of seeing our interdependence and eschews any concept of an entirely separate self.

With the help of postmodernism, Buddhism, and Jung, I wend my way through the thickets of conscious and unconscious meanings that have grown up in today's world around the issues of gender and desire among women and men. I hope that you will find the journey an adventure and that the drama of its development may change your mind.

Acknowledgments

Without David Rosen and the Fay Lecture Series, this book would not exist. It was through his kind invitation that I began to pursue, more seriously than I had in the past, several topics that I had explored less formally over the years. I always am struggling to make analytical psychology as useful as possible, both in the world of depth psychology and in society at large. The Fay Lectures gave me an opportunity to do this with a new audience of students, professionals, laypeople, and professors.

What I had not counted on when I accepted the invitation to lecture in 1996 was the overflowing generosity, enthusiasm, engagement, and intelligence of the people in College Station who support these lectures. Texas A&M University, the Department of Psychology, the Department of Women's Studies, and various university officials could not have been better hosts or a better audience. Dr. Rosen and Carolyn Fay in particular made me feel not only at home but also like an old friend. In fact, by the end of three days of lectures, dinners, and parties, I felt as if I had been among my College Station friends for years and could not imagine that our encounter had been so brief. It is hard to convey in words the lively spirit of inquiry and support that surrounds this series. I am more grateful than I can express for this opportunity to see analytical psychology functioning so well in an academic setting.

I also had fine support from Dr. Rosen and Texas A&M University Press in assembling this manuscript for a book. Dr. Rosen is a first-rate editor, and I appreciate his help in fine-tuning the text. My own research assistant, Carol Foltz, was invaluable, too, in helping me make this book the scholarly work it should be.

My husband, Ed Epstein, heard the first reading of the four Fay lectures in our living room. As usual, he helped weed out boring references to my favorite philosophers and reduce certain academic comments to a necessary brevity. The aspect of his participation that I enjoyed most, however, was his presence in College Station, Texas. Together we felt so welcomed and embraced there that we proudly wore our Texas A&M tee shirts upon our return home.

In acknowledging the warm welcome and intelligent conversations offered by those I encountered in the course of my Fay Lectures, I want to indicate how grateful I am for the opportunity to write this book in such a supportive atmosphere. Of course, I take full responsibility for its flaws. It is my hope that this volume will provide a new way of looking at some of the issues we face as we struggle to reduce our self-protection and projective views of the opposite sex.

Gender
&
Desire

CHAPTER ONE

The Problem of Realism in Analytical Psychology

In talking about the nature of gender and desire, we shall be entering some dark and heavily wooded terrain. Thus I decided to begin with something light: a little parable about reality—about philosophies of reality, even—that illustrates some important differences in how we believe that we come to know ourselves and the world.

> Three baseball umpires are arguing about how they call balls and strikes and who is best at it. The first one says, "I calls 'em as I sees 'em." The second, hoping to top the first, says, "I calls 'em as they are." The third, after listening politely, says triumphantly, "They ain't nothin' till I calls 'em!"

In these three voices,[1] we can hear three different versions of truth. The first umpire reports only what is seen. This umpire is an *empiricist*, reporting on what happens "out there" as honestly and completely as possible. The first definition of *empiricism* in the *Webster's Ninth Collegiate Dictionary* (1985) is "a former school of medical practice founded on experience without the aid of science or theory." When medicine was purely empirical, it was observational only. Empiricists cannot say why things happen; they can say only what they can see.

The second voice is that of a *naïve realist*, someone who *knows* exactly how things are. To me, "I calls 'em as they are" sounds like certain contemporary biological psychiatrists, sociobiologists, and geneticists who tell us exactly why we are the way we are. Every day we hear about yet another trait or illness that is "located on" a certain gene. We can be persuaded that we are determined by our genes and hormones, by our brain structures and biochemistry. When we hear that depression is "really" a biochemical imbalance, we are getting a realist version of depression. When we believe that criminality and alcoholism are "really" genetic diseases, we are engaging in modern realism. A sociobiologist claims that men seek multiple sexual partners while women prefer monogamy, and asserts that this is so because men can produce greater numbers of progeny than women can. That is a realist account of polygamy.[2]

For realists, our experiences, sensations, and impressions are not all of the same value. Only a hierarchy of mental functions—with rational processes at the top—will guide us to truth, allowing us to discriminate a perception from a hallucination, validity from error, memory from fantasy. Other scientists, especially macro- and micro-level physicists, are more modest and circumspect, claiming that their perspective is relative to their point of view. But the realists—those who believe that they have uncovered the truth about human nature—get more media coverage.

The third umpire's voice at first sounds like that of a *naïve subjectivist*, someone who believes that truth is constituted in the telling or the naming of it, someone who may have only a single perspective on what is happening. Such a voice opens the possibility that there is no world independent of our involvement in it, our experience of it. There is no reality "out there." Without us human beings, there is no game in town.

These three voices illustrate three perspectives that overlap and inform each other in contemporary psychological theories. We could call them the premodern, modern, and postmodern. The *premodern* view is that knowledge based upon observation is truth;

there is no understanding of how the observer may contribute to an observation. When we defend ourselves by claiming that our experience is ample justification for truth, without any awareness of how we might be shaping that experience, then we are premodern empiricists.

The *modern* view of truth acknowledges that the human mind plays a part in reality, allowing or blocking access to the truth. Certain kinds of mental processes or methods appear to lead to a predictable, reliable, and stable truth. In modernity, we discover that rational, logical, and mathematical methods can be used to operate on the world around us and increase our competence and control. Some kinds of thinking appear to lead to the truth, while others seem to obscure it. Inductive and deductive reasoning can lead to a predictable, coherent reality; but intuition, metaphor, and imagination lead to dangerous half-truths that obscure what actually is knowable about our world.[3]

The *postmodern* view is yet another view of truth. It proceeds from the premise that any account of truth (whether scientific or intuitive) originates with a person (or a community of people) and reflects personal assumptions, emotions, and meanings. Even our most highly developed scientific methods are only the best we can do for the moment in attempting to be objective or unbiased in our views.

According to postmodernists, we never can hope to get beyond or outside human interpretation. Our most advanced scientific methods will always be fallible, limited, and constrained because the involvement and limitations of human consciousness are inescapable in whatever we study. We never will encounter a truth that stands apart from ourselves and our interpretation of the matter under consideration. Consequently we cannot know a world "out there." We can know only the human construction of the world.

We are engaged continuously in constructing, out of our perceptions, emotions, and cognitions, a world of space, time, and causality. Ours is a world under active construction. Because of this, it is constrained by inescapable limitations, no matter how much we strive to get around them. Our reality is incomplete and fallible, because we are neither omniscient nor omnipotent.

This human reality is not solipsistic or arbitrary, though.[4] We are engaged with *something*, but we cannot know that something directly. More important, the ways in which we engage and make a world have universal characteristics.[5] Our agreement as individuals about the world we perceive forms the basis of our shared existence as a species. As embodied, emotional, and languaged creatures, we depend upon each other and upon a diverse environment to construct the world that we perceive. None of us is an independent, isolated mind, captured only by an imagination; yet none of us can know a "real world" directly.

All three of these versions of truth are used in contemporary psychological practice. As theorists and practitioners, we are balanced and well informed if we attend to all three of them, recognizing that their logics exist in a nested arrangement. At the first level is premodern truth, which is encompassed and reorganized by modernism, which in turn is encompassed and reorganized by postmodernism. To put this another way, the first level of knowledge is experience, the next is discrimination and ordering of types of experience, and the third is accounting for the origins and limitations of our knowledge and experience.

This third level is relatively new among Western theories of knowledge, being, in its current form, only about twenty-five or thirty years old. Although major elements of postmodernism are to be found in Buddhist and other Asian teachings, in Western philosophy the logical demonstrations of the position were developed only recently. Modernity led to postmodernism, as the limits of rational and mathematical methods became logically apparent. This revelation first was captured in the philosophy of science, as modern physics began to grapple with problems and make discoveries concerning relativism and quantum mechanics. Like the next

stage in any developmental sequence, postmodernism has thrown
into question much of what, in modernity, we took to be simply
true—especially realist assumptions about ourselves and the
world.

In what follows, I develop the idea that analytical psychology can
be informed and illuminated by particular kinds of postmodern
thinking: hermeneutics and constructivism. I show how these
methods have helped me overcome the realism that haunts aspects
of our theory. Although Jung was not by any means a realist, he was
a product of modernity.[6] Because he could not escape his *Weltan-
schauung*, he had a tendency to view his major ideas as realities
beyond human interpretation. Analytical psychology, in conse-
quence, has suffered from problems inherent in realism, and these
sometimes have interfered with its clinical usefulness and made it
seem antiquated and authoritarian.

I also show how analytical psychology informs and illuminates
postmodernism. The integration of analytical psychology with
certain aspects of postmodernism opens new vistas in understanding gender, myth, and desire, in personal, clinical, and cultural set-
tings. In order to show how this works, first (in this chapter) I
differentiate three branches of postmodernism, explaining why
I believe that hermeneutics and constructivism correct the problems posed by realism, and harmonize with Jungian psychology. I
also set forth my own postmodern Jungian understanding of archetype and complex. Briefly I explain my understanding of living
mythology as a form of realism in everyday life and hint at how the
movement from myth to metaphor works in human development.
This latter shift is treated more fully in the final chapter of
this book.

In the second chapter, I give a depth-psychological account of
gender and self from a postmodern Jungian perspective, aided by
some aspects of Buddhist psychology that deepen the postmodern
context. I explore the apparently unlikely pairing of Jung's psy-

chology and feminism, explaining why I find them congenial mates, fertile in producing a framework for interpreting desire, projection, and opposites in intrapsychic and interpersonal aspects of sex differences.

Then, with all this as background, I examine a fragment of a myth that is alive symbolically in symptoms, art, leisure, and love: the story of Pandora, in Greek mythology the first woman, who brings mortality to humans. Looking at the Pandora story from both clinical and cultural viewpoints, we may approach the topics of gender, myth, psychological complex, and desire with a postmodern sensibility. Here we focus especially on the problem of being "the object of desire."

In the final chapter, I return to our earlier discussion of gender and self, to suggest in a more nuanced way how to transform myth into metaphor. This synthesis of Jung and postmodernism concludes with an account of being "the subject of desire." I hope to persuade you that thinking in postmodern terms enlivens the perspective of analytical psychology and extends it in the direction in which Jung himself was taking it at the time of his death in 1961. At the same time, I hope to show that a serious study of universals, such as archetype and emotion, vastly furthers our knowledge of human interpretation and development.

Postmodernism and Analytical Psychology

We are living in a time that is markedly different from the one in which Carl Jung lived and died. Although he lived long into the twentieth century, Jung did not live long enough to encounter the sweeping philosophical and social critique called "postmodernism." Harbingers of postmodernism appeared in the last three decades of Jung's life: submolecular physics, structuralism, evolutionary theory, ethology, and developmental psychology all contributed to what eventually became a serious critique of our claims for truth in science, history, and morality.

It will become clear that I am encouraged by certain aspects of postmodernism, although I do not endorse or agree with all of its branches. My optimism stems from the fact that two branches of postmodernism have been profoundly useful in my clinical work and everyday life. Hermeneutics (the theory of interpretation and understanding) and constructivism (the philosophy ensuing from the premise that we actively construe our reality) have allowed me to clarify the assumptions I make in holding certain theories about people and their lives. These branches of postmodernism have opened up a whole new way of looking at my own knowledge system, enhancing my empathy and compassion for those whose realities differ from my own. These forms of postmodernism have allowed me to send down a taproot from my ideas to my experiences, and to see where my thinking is inconsistent with my actions and attitudes.

Without this framework, I doubt that I could have continued my work as an analytical psychologist. During my training to become an analyst, I reluctantly acknowledged major areas of discomfort with Jung's theories. I found that I had serious philosophical and ethical problems with certain assumptions that increasingly seemed elitist, sexist, and Eurocentric. In sum, I was disturbed by tendencies toward stereotyping and reductionism.

With the advent of feminism in the 1970s and postmodernism in the 1980s, I began to clarify my vague doubts and develop a formal critique of aspects of our theory. This critique has allowed me to reengage with analytical psychology; in my view, the latter is more consistent and powerful when problems with realism are cleared up. Among these problems is a strong tendency to make things—substances or essences—out of passing moods or states; in philosophy this process is called *reification*. This is a form of realism, because it assumes that certain states or experiences tell us how things really are, beyond human interpretation. At times reification can lead to typing people according to certain ways of being. For example, "Thinking Type," "Extravert," "too rational," and "animus-possessed" are labels often used pejoratively in Jungian circles. Although I never have exemplified those categories myself, I often have been tagged with those labels, apparently because of my interest in understanding theory. On Jungian type-tests, I consistently scored as an Introverted Intuitive with a strong Feeling function, but in Jungian groups I regularly was asked if I was an Extraverted Thinker. These queries permitted me to see how easily we could reify a function (my interest in theory, in this case) turning it into a thing used to label a person.

In regard to the archetypes of Masculine and Feminine, Jungian theory often seemed caught up in reductive dichotomization of the two sexes into almost symmetrical opposites. The archetypal Masculine was described as a principle of Logos, rationality, culture, autonomy—as epitomized in the myth of the Hero and/or in accounts or critiques of the ego. The Masculine was connected with action, authority, and light. The archetypal Feminine, by contrast, was described as Eros, connectedness, nature, relationship—as epitomized in accounts and critiques of anima or in typologies of goddesses. The Feminine was connected with receptivity, nature, and darkness.

I found these accounts of gender enormously problematical, in that they seemed to prescribe what was natural for members of each sex over the lifespan. I need not detail here what the traditional Jungian narrative of men's and women's lives described as a "healthy" lifespan. What was so troubling was a tendency to substantialize or reify what are passing states in everyone's experience—times of separateness and connectedness, of reproductive passions and creative insights, of achievement and dependence. Making gendered labels and categories out of passing states often reduced people to ideas, rather than meeting people with curiosity and empathy and attempting to understand how and why they see themselves as they do.

In addition to this typing of genders, there was the problem of characterizing the core of our subjectivity as the archetype of the Self. This archetype, rather than being used as a hypothetical construct for a particular function, often was described as a person with its own intentions, reasons, and desires. Many discussions of the Self seemed to me to make a "thing" out of a no-thing. From a close reading of Jung's own Self theory, I realized that his lasting intention was to give a name to the central organizing function of personality, a name that would allow us to study this function. Jung's goal seemed to me to be identical with that of the developmentalist, Jean Piaget, who also had a term designating a function of transcendent unity and coherence in the universe, a function manifest also in the individual.[7] Piaget used the term "epistemic subject" to designate the same function that Jung called by the term "Self." Piaget warned his followers against seeing this as related to the "individual subject"—the person. There should be no equating the person and the epistemic subject, because the latter was a hypothesis based on inferences about structure. Jung used the familiar term "self" to refer to the same function; it became tempting to describe this function as if it were a person.

As chapter 2 indicates, Jung's concept of Self evolved in several stages. Earlier, its characteristics resembled the notion of the individual soul more than they did those of Piaget's epistemic subject. Later, Jung talked about the Self more as a central organizing function, an empty center, similar to Piaget's notion of a transcendent coherence.

In addition to these specific problems with analytical psychology, when I became acquainted with postmodernism, I began to question claims that I or anyone else might make for something being universal in human life. As a Jungian, I was claiming that archetypes are universal, that the Self is similar in all human beings, and that everyone has an inner theater made up of persona, shadow, ego, wise old people, tricksters, and anima or animus. How universal could all this be?

My own understanding (and anxiety) began to clear up, as the nature of human interpretation became clearer to me. Through reading and discussing postmodern philosophy and theory—beginning with Heidegger and Wittgenstein; continuing through Gadamer, Harré, Quine, Rorty, Charles Taylor, and many other philosophers of action and interpretation; and including a number of critiques of psychoanalytic theory and practices (e.g., Jane Flax, Stephen Mitchell, Roy Schafer, Donald Spence, and others)—I found a name for the crisis I was experiencing.[8]

It was a crisis of modern realism, parading through the claims made by modern Jungians and, indeed, to some extent those made by Jung himself. What may be confusing is that Jung's thought often has been dubbed "idealism." Certain kinds of idealism (such as Platonic idealism) suffer also from a realist bias, a conviction that one can "call 'em as they are." When an archetype is understood as a force or essence that exists outside or beyond human interpretation, there arises the realist belief that we can call 'em as they are. We sound like we have Psychological Truth at our fingertips.

This way of thinking produces, among other things, a certain grandiosity in theorizing. People begin to sound like God, or they make Jung into a god; they speak with an air of *knowing*.

Although on many occasions Jung cautioned against this kind of speaking, within his theory there is a problem that seems to invite speaking as from on high, as if one had an infallible source of knowledge. This problem arises, as I mentioned earlier, in speaking as if one could know "what the Self is thinking"—even *that* the Self is thinking! Here is a random example from a well-regarded contemporary book on dream interpretation: "A man dreamt, 'I am a lion.' This presented his Self's view of a potential lion force." If the Self is a concept inferred from an unknowable, transcendent coherence in the personality, it cannot have a view. It is not a person.

What hermeneutics helped me see were the mistakes in our knowledge system that made it seem as if we were not interpreting at all but were reading signs from an omniscient source. Analytical psychology, like any other depth psychology, is a body of theory and practice whose boundaries and domain reflect the (approximate) agreement of a community of experts about how to understand conscious and unconscious human life.

In our community, no clear agreement exists concerning our central concept of Self. Some Jungians regard it as equivalent to the soul or God, whereas others regard it as a principle of organization. These two views are substantially different and often mutually exclusive. I count myself in the latter group, regarding the Self as a principle of coherence or unity that transcends the individual self and is inferred through human experience.

The problem of realism in analytical psychology has not yet been resolved, although I resolved my own identity crisis (whether or not I can call myself Jungian) when I learned what the problem was and that there are many good solutions to it. I can see my way to revise theoretical inconsistencies in Jung's later work in order to bring analytical psychology in line with contemporary hermeneutics. I also can understand and answer my colleagues in psychoanalysis who dismiss Jung and Jungians as "essentialists" or "foundationalists." For example, in 1991, a psychiatrist reviewing a book I wrote with Florence Wiedemann generally was positive about our clinical theory and methods but extremely critical of our use of Jung's psychology. He criticized analytical psychology for being "steeped . . . in phylogenetic, mystical authoritarianism."[9]

If the reviewer were here in person, I could respond to him now, understanding where we have been unable to see the limits of our theory. When we speak as if meaning is discovered, not constructed, as if it arises from archetypes and layers of the unconscious, rather than from human beings engaged with each other and a world in flux, then we are essentialists.[10] If we believe that archetypes organize us and the physical world, that they exist in our bodies or genes or in the physical objects around us, we are realists. We lose track of the fact that this whole interpretive system is created by us, that it emerges from our understanding and not directly from our biology or the physical world.

My own grasp of analytical psychology—its theory and practice—always was nonessentialist, even before I knew the term. Perhaps because I came to analytical psychology with a background in Buddhist practice and knowledge, or perhaps because I had participated in some human liberation movements, I never thought that Jung was a realist, even when I could see that he used some essentialist reasoning. Obviously it was difficult for Jung to step outside of his own *Zeitgeist;* he, like Freud, was steeped in the scientific realism of modernity. Jung worked very hard not to be bound by that system, however, and in many ways he succeeded.

In my view, Jung was moving ineluctably toward a certain type of postmodern thinking that strongly resembles contemporary hermeneutics and certain aspects of psychological constructivism.[11] I believe that Jung's ideas about the nature of "reality"—that it depends upon universal aspects of the human psyche—presaged a lot of thinking now going on among some psychologists and psychoanalysts who more and more are coming to see that much of what we have taken to be "perception" is highly interpretive, based on emotional, relational, and cultural factors.

Researchers and theorists of infant development (e.g., Beatrice Beebe, J. D. Lichtenberg, Daniel Stern, and others) have documented how the exquisite interplay between child and parent helps the infant construct a world.[12] Similarly, researchers of human emotions (e.g., Izard, Tompkins, Lewis) have demonstrated the universality of those emotions[13]—described as situational systems of motivation and response or even as "emotional intelligence."[14]

Such emotional intelligence, with its unconscious images and response systems, is thought to circumvent the cortex in directing us to assume, perceive, and act in certain ways, based upon our adaptation to an original emotional environment. At the core of this primary human intelligence is a powerful predisposition to form coherent action-image sequences that, without revising Jung's later definition of the term, could be called *archetypes.* For example, Jung wrote in 1955:

This term is not meant to denote an inherited idea, but rather an in-
herited mode of psychic functioning, corresponding to the inborn way
in which the chick emerges from the egg, the bird builds its nest, a cer-
tain kind of wasp stings the motor ganglion of the caterpillar, and eels
find their way to the Bermudas. This aspect of the archetype, the
purely biological one, is the proper concern of scientific psychology.[15]

This ethological definition of archetype, typical of Jung's later
work, is complemented by his clinical descriptions of the awe-
some emotion associated with archetypal images and enactments.
There is a strong parallel between Jung's account and the one
given by Daniel Goleman.[16]

Jung's discoveries over the years, from his early empirical work
on the association experiment to his later cross-cultural and inter-
disciplinary scholarly research, returned again and again to the importance of subjectivity, the experience of the human subject, in
shaping what we call "reality."

Some of my colleagues regard postmodernism and multicultur-
alism with suspicion, viewing them as the newest products of the
academic ivory tower. To the contrary, I have found in these
movements a return to the practical, through the recognition that
practices shape theories and not the reverse. To complete this discussion of the merits of postmodernism, however, I want to distinguish between two types of postmodernism in the social sciences,
"skeptical" and "affirmative."[17]

The skeptical type of postmodernism I generally have found to
be inconsistent with analytical psychology.[18] Deconstruction and
its allies are the mainstays of skepticism. Originated by French
philosopher Jacques Derrida, deconstruction tends to undermine
any belief in universals.[19] To "deconstruct" a belief or concept, one
takes apart the assumptions that underlie the key terms of that system. Whatever these assumptions are (often they are called "truth
claims"), they will be seen as resting on somebody's pet ideas and
ideals—tied to the privilege or advantage that somebody has over

somebody else. For instance, in arguments that favor underlying biological differences between the sexes, a deconstructionist will point to the absence of any account of similarities between the sexes (of which there are many), and to the author's failure to reveal her or his biases. Deconstructionists analyze by examining what is not said, what is left out. They maintain that any claim to truth also is a claim to power. Therefore, they would say that civilizations and knowledge are primarily defenses of the privileged and powerful. Those who are less privileged are left out of truth, except as they are regarded from the perspectives of the privileged.

I shall not go into more detail here, except to say that, while aspects of deconstruction can be useful in scrutinizing what is missing in an account, overall this is a rather cynical philosophy that I find very problematical. Much of deconstruction is composed of taking apart old cultural biases and beliefs and examining how they were motivated. The approach leaves us with a picture of human beings as isolated little islands of individual meaning, with little that can be trusted to connect us to one another or anything else.

On the other hand, the affirmative branches of postmodernism—hermeneutics and constructivism—advance theories that include the idea of universals in human life. These universals are exemplified by our embodiment, emotions, cognitions, and perceptions. Often these factors are described as "constraints" upon our ability to see and know things, but these constraints result in our sharing a consensual world. Here is how philosopher Charles Taylor (1995) describes it. Ours is a "'world shaped' by embodiment in the sense that the way of experiencing or living the world is essentially that of an agent with this particular kind of body."[20] Our active engagement with others and the environment—through actions, perceptions, emotions, thoughts—shapes what we take to be the phenomenal world. This embodiment is not the same thing as biology, nor can it be reduced narrowly to the knowledge or methods of biology. Our embodiment is a primary imprint, an archetype, of what it is to be human. There is nothing that comes to us without our involvement in it; that is the kind of beings we are. And for this reason, we never really can "call 'em as they are."

Constraints and Archetypes

The constraints of being human can be studied and investigated; they are the structures through which we operate in formulating human values, truths, reality. The formal definition of archetype is "primary imprint." Jung initially used the idea of archetype in a way which now seems essentialist, to mean a primary imago or image; but later he revised it to mean a motivational system, like an "innate releasing mechanism," the term originally used by Tinbergen.[21]

Jung was interested in tracing the patterned responses of human life—the constraints of our embodiment—in order to discover that which transcended the merely personal. In his later definition of archetype, he described it as the predisposition to form a coherent image in an emotionally aroused state, something he called a "situational pattern." In such an aroused state, we all have the inherent tendency to form an image with positive or negative emotional potentials. All human beings, the world over, are organized by archetypes or motivational systems that are expressed in images such as Great and Terrible Mother, Great and Terrible Father, gods and goddesses, tricksters and divine children; these recur in folk and fairy tales, religions, and mythologies. But these images do not arise from some substrate outside human experience, some mystical or ideal reality. Rather, they arise from the constraints of being human, from being as limited and dependent as we are. Without ample knowledge of these constraints, we can be misled into thinking that we are fundamentally individual, unique, even unknowable.

Constructivism, the belief that we actively construe the world, has helped me understand Jung's theory of archetypes in terms of universal constraints attendant upon human embodiment. This word *constraint* clarifies the resistance that many of us have to understanding the power of archetype. As a simple example, take a twenty-nine-year-old man who comes to see me for psychotherapy because he is uncertain about his career choice. He is in graduate school preparing for a profession, but he wonders if the profession is "right" for him. Although he already has invested considerable effort in his chosen field, he has problems making a commitment to it. He does not merely wonder, but he frets and worries, he ruminates and obsesses, on the details of his own and others' career choices. In no way does he want to hear that there is something "universal" or impersonal about his dilemma. He sees this as a very personal issue.

How do I evaluate his symptoms? I know that, in our society, adulthood begins to be felt as a serious demand around the age of twenty-eight. If, by this time, a young person has no clear commitment to work or relationship, that person begins to feel profoundly uncomfortable. The period from twenty-eight to thirty years of age is an initiation time fraught with dangerous images. Although the age for this passage varies considerably from society to society, in all societies there is a point after which young people are expected to leave adolescence and join other adults in the activities that support society. If they fail, there are serious consequences—explicit or implicit.

So I did not consider this young man's anxiety to be only neurotic. Although there was a neurotic component, it also was developmental, related to his phase in the lifespan. He, however, would resist thinking that he was in a "stage" that exemplified anything. When I speak of "phase" or "stage" here, I am referring to a period of the lifespan when certain tasks are to be accomplished. My usage is not to be confused with "stage theories" such as those of Piaget or Loevinger. The chronological age at which a certain phase occurs varies from culture to culture, and from subculture to subculture in our society. As embodied, languaged, and social beings, we transit some predictable landscapes during the human lifespan, even though timing may shift from group to group.

You may balk at my strong belief that certain aspects of development are universal, that we live within certain constraints as human beings. After all, you say, are not development and greater consciousness about greater and greater freedom? Yes. But freedom is, in large part, the ability to recognize constraint, in order to function well within the limits of that which constrains us. Freedom almost always involves responsibility; in the case of archetypes, it is a responsibility to see what it means to be human, quite apart from what it feels like to be a person.

I never suppose that I have the final say or the ultimate knowledge concerning archetypes or how human constraints may operate in an individual's life. I always assume that my knowledge gradually will change over time, but I also believe in the value of studying and theorizing about what is universal—emotions, archetypes, attachment bonds—using the methods and concepts we have available.

Whereas constructivism examines how we construe a world, the other affirmative discipline of postmodernism, hermeneutics, looks more at how we arrive at knowledge and truth. Later, I shall employ a feminist form of hermeneutics to look at how and why we see gender differences as we do.

Psychological Complexes and Mythology

Before we leave this introduction to a postmodern view of archetype, I want to mention one other way in which the idea of archetype is very important in a contemporary analysis of emotional life: its participation in psychological disorders and distress. Jung's later theory unites the idea of a "collective unconscious" (which is universal) with that of a "personal unconscious" (which is individual) in the concept of a psychological complex.[22]

After roughly 1944, Jung refers to psychological complexes as being organized around an archetype.[23] Intensely arousing emotional images, such as the primordial Great and Terrible Mothers of infancy, lead us to develop emotionally based memories and motivations. Emotional intelligence, as means by which we have adapted to our original environment, has a different psychological and neurological basis than does practical or abstract reasoning.[24] Although an individual may become adept in using practice and abstract thought, and in using practical reasoning, that same individual may be infantile or childish in emotional intelligence.

Psychological complexes are the structures of emotional intelligence: they are the residues of the original ways in which we tried to come to terms with the interpersonal-emotional world that surrounded us. One reason why neurosis and other more disabling psychological disorders are so deeply motivating is that they express complexes to which we are strongly committed because they are the underpinnings of our interpersonal reality.

Think back to infancy. We now know that each of us spent some time as an overwhelmed, enraged, unattended little bundle of nerves. No parent (or team of parents) is so well attuned and so constantly available as to never frustrate an infant. And, of course, frustration is necessary for development. In an infantile state of frustration, we all formed images of a Terrible Mother, of a caregiver (male or female) upon whom we depended, who sometimes was not available, who was preoccupied or intruded on us painfully. There are smells, sounds, colors, and kinesthetic components of such an emotionally charged image. All of us have archetypal images of a Terrible Mother; she is universal. And yet the circumstances of a particular life—the presence or absence of effective mothering, attunement or the lack of it, and so on—will color this archetype and give it weight and substance as a personal psychological complex.

Such a Terrible Mother complex will recur repeatedly over a lifetime whenever the cues are present. Hear certain sounds, see certain things, and all the emotions surrounding this frightening image will motivate us to reenact what seems to be reality. As adolescents or adults, we can enact both the "subject" and the "object" poles of a complex—in this case, the roles of Victim Child and Terrible Mother.

Psychological complexes are transferred or projected onto, or repeated with, our partners, our children, our therapists, and our bosses, much more often than with our friends, our neighbors, or strangers.[25] Whenever we sense that we are locked in, unable to escape the influence of another, we tend to be drawn back into the emotional intelligence of our early lives when escape was impossible. And so the child who perceived his mother as depressed, weak, and empty will tend to perceive his wife in the same way if she cries, complains, or criticizes in a way that sounds like Mother. The old situational pattern will be superimposed on the new relationship.

The reason that Jung's theory of psychological complexes is so important to postmodernism is that it includes the idea of an archetypal core. Jung's theory alerts us to the fact that we all create great and terrible parent complexes and many other psychic realities—and that they are not easy to reason away. These complexes become pathological when they overtake our current reality too frequently or too powerfully, either because they were formed under traumatic conditions (leaving consciousness very weakened) or because later life events conspire to reduce our ego functioning.

At times, we all are neurotic or mood-disordered or even psychotic (in dreams, for instance) because psychological complexes arise in us. We all have multiple personalities—several competing subjectivities. This latter characteristic of human emotional life is universal and indicates that we are multilayered beings marked by embodiment. This embodiment includes archetypes that organize the ways of reproduction, the course of a human lifespan, our dependence upon others for reflections of ourselves, and the knowledge and inevitability of our deaths.

Over millennia, mythology has developed narratives about archetypal images and psychological complexes, about the universal constraints and conditions of being human. Although mythology has served many functions for societies and cultures, a major function it continues to serve is that of illustrating the meanings of collective human situations.

When a mythology is alive, it forms the basis of what we call "reality." Only when a myth is dying—in the sense of no longer seeming to be real—can it be used as metaphor to illustrate something else. When a myth is dying, we can stand apart from it and see it as meaning something. The myth of Demeter and Persephone, for example, is alive when a person is trapped in a terrible history of child sexual abuse, in which the mother is imagined to have ignored what was being done by a father, stepfather, or uncle in perverting the developing sexuality of a young daughter. We find the living images of this myth in the fantasies and dreams of such a Persephone daughter. The myth becomes a "story about" an abduction only when it no longer is alive.

The living myth of our time is scientific realism. It is the basis of what we use to constitute what is true and worthy of belief. We normally approach the findings of our most respected sciences with reverent belief, not with skepticism. The most captivating current scientific myths are genetics, astrophysics, neuroscience, and subatomic physics. The tales told in these myths are amazing, yet we take them at face value. When I read the Sunday *New York Times*, I expect to see some articles about how moods, talents, beliefs, or desires are rooted in our genes. Very few people question the implications of thinking in terms of genetics—what is lost to us as well as what might be gained—because most of us believe that genetics reveal the truth.

Some people question whether science is a myth, either because they are realists and separate scientific fact from myth, or because they do not believe that science carries enough emotional and spiritual significance to be considered a myth. Certainly Jung believed that science was our myth when he called it the "spiritual adventure of our age."[26] Science is the grand story of our epoch, unfolding our worldview before us day by day, explaining natural phenomena, our practices, and our beliefs. We have not transcended it, but, through postmodernism, we have come to its boundaries. To study dying myths, to use their metaphors to understand ourselves, reveals something of the universal in human life, and it also allows us to recognize the power of myth itself in providing that grand story that we take to be reality.

From all that I have learned about human development, through research and theory and the practice of psychotherapy, I would say that we must understand the fundamental workings of our own emotions, through our complexes and their archetypes, in order to know ourselves. Without this account of what is universal, we are likely to feel alienated and adrift, isolated and fundamentally separate—a fairly accurate description of the human being as a deconstructed self.

Yet if we claim our knowledge from a realist perspective—asserting that we "calls 'em as they are"—we err in the inflated belief that we can get a God's-eye view of Truth, that somehow we can step outside human (i.e., constrained) interpretation. This is why analytical psychology is strengthened by affirmative postmodernism. It keeps us modest—alert to the limitations of our knowledge and aware of the consequences of our theories. At the same time, postmodernism is strengthened through the inclusion of universals in its accounts of personal life. When discussions of constructivism or hermeneutics sound as if each person is alone and separate, unable to make *any* claim of universal morality, human welfare, human development, and the like—then a theory of archetypes and complexes is a needed antidote.

The next chapter applies postmodern Jungian understanding to the question of how we construct gender: What does it mean to have a self of one gender and to call the other the "opposite"? I hope to show how a specifically feminist orientation to an application of analytical psychology opens up many new avenues in understanding symptoms, actions, archetypes, and myth. When we then examine the Greek myth of the first woman, Pandora, we shall be able to say something about how Woman was constructed in ancient times and how she continues to be known. Pandora, like Eve, brings mortality into the human world. What Woman brings into the world is death—a curious reversal of the fact that women bring life and birth, but one clearly relevant to the meaning of Woman in a patriarchal world, whether that of the Greeks or our own.

CHAPTER TWO

Gender, Contrasexuality, and Self

Whenever I speak about gender in a Jungian context, I feel compelled to present a good deal of background material concerning the way I think about the psychological and sociocultural implications of this enormous topic. Too often among Jungian audiences I encounter a realist tendency to believe that Masculinity and Femininity are universal archetypes through which our bodies and nature come into being, according to our biological sex.

Not too long ago, I was speaking at a Jungian conference, making a plea for a feminist, constructivist approach to gender and sex differences, and a well-meaning participant asked me a question about an adolescent girl's dream. In the dream, the girl saw herself with a bloody wound in her neck. The girl recently had started menstruating, and my questioner said, "Isn't this an indication of the girl's problems with femininity?" I answered with a caveat about not assuming what femininity or a menstrual period might *mean* to an individual, noting that I could not say much about the dream without knowing a lot more about the girl, about when she had this dream, other images in the dream, and her view of her recent menstruation. My questioner was aghast. "Isn't menstruation universally a *feminine* event? Doesn't biology precede language? Surely menstruation is archetypal."

I replied that "biology" does not precede anything, being a set of scientific principles and methods, a field of study used by humans to predict and understand various aspects of our own and others' biophysical nature. Further, menstruation, to be sure, is a universal occurrence among female people, arousing strong emotions, and so is archetypal. But the meanings associated with menstruation vary from one society to another, from one subculture to another, and even from one person to another. I do not believe that it always means something that we would consider "feminine." I feel sure that it could, for instance, signal attributes that we might consider "masculine" from a traditional perspective: greater autonomy and freedom from Mother, newfound power of the body and the reproductive system, sexual prowess, and the like. In other words, the fact that menstruation is a universal physical event for (almost all) female people does not imply that it has a universal meaning.

What follows next is a discussion of sex, gender, and embodiment. It deals with the psychological meanings associated with the construct of an Opposite Sex and helps clarify the nature of archetype and meaning.

Gender and Difference

Universally, the human community is divided into two sexes, marked by signs and symbols of gender. This fact has great psychological significance in our lives as individuals, couples, and groups. Each of us is born into an ongoing narrative about our own sex and the opposite sex, a story that will constrain and engender possibilities for action and identity, for self-image and sexuality. Each of us will form strong internal images of femininity and masculinity, around which we will create fantasies, life stories, romance, and antagonism. While we identify with one gender, we develop an unconscious complex around the Other. This subjective Other, this so-called opposite, will mark the boundaries of who we can become. The Other plays a major role in everyone's theory of self, becoming a defense through projection, and becoming a belief that there are many human beings with whom we have limited similarity.

In the way I am speaking about gender, I differentiate it from sex (as in sex differences). The sex we are born as and the gender we become are not the same thing, although one flows from the other. Sex is a matter of embodiment: structural and functional properties of the human body, including hormones and brain functions, that provide the biological foundation of certain physical attributes. Most of these relate to reproduction, but there are some sex differences—such as expectable differences in mortality rates between male and female infants, and the greater average longevity of the female—that apparently are independent of reproduction.

Arriving here in a particular embodiment, as male or female, is a limitation that we cannot escape. Our sexual embodiment will develop into certain opportunities, such as giving birth or having a penis, and constraints, as we are limited to *only* certain potentials and actualities. Even when people have a so-called "sex change" operation, they are not able to break through this limitation of embodiment; they can mutilate the body, but they never can change it fully into one belonging to the opposite sex.

Gender, on the other hand, is very mutable and flexible. It is the identity club into which we are assigned at birth, when our bodies are read by the elders who say whether we are female or male. Gender is the meaning system, the narrative or story that says what each sex means, what roles should be played and why. All societies have only two gender clubs, so gender creates both a division among human beings and a division within the psyche, between what is called "self" and what is regarded as its "opposite."

Gender usually is assigned at birth, but now it is possible to be assigned and given a gendered name *before* birth, as parents, through a variety of prenatal tests, can determine the sex of infants as yet unborn. "What a pretty girl!" "What a strong boy!" "How sweet she is!" "How smart he is!" These are the kinds of stories that begin to be told at birth and continue to mark each of us for a life-time.[1]

Whereas sex is inflexible and inescapable, gender is flexible. It varies from culture to culture, from family to family, and even from peer group to peer group, as well as changing in meaning over a single individual's lifetime.[2] For example, among North American adolescents and young adults, apparel can cover such a wide gender range that young people can look gender-neutral. Some young Americans believe strongly in gender flexibility and wear clothes or behave such that it is difficult to know which gender they are. Other young Americans, in contrast, adopt fairly rigidly gendered appearances, attempting especially to appeal to the opposite sex through traditional expressions of sexual attractiveness. Over a lifetime, the individual also may change her or his ideas of what being male or female means. For instance, a midlife woman going to graduate school may believe that women are more competent and better organized than men, whereas in high school the same woman may have believed that girls were not as smart or as capable as boys.

Gender begins with what society, culture, and family have expected of each sex, and, as we discover that these expectations are more flexible than we at first thought, we start to examine the nature of gender itself. None of us can escape gender definitions, because we live in a highly gendered world, although some aspects of gender roles are changing every day and major changes have been made during the past twenty-five years. We all have conscious or unconscious fantasies of escaping gender definitions, or so I believe.

What we may see as prototypical differences between women and men are not archetypal or universal. They are cultural and social. Often people say that nurturance must be a biological component of women's nature, because women bear and nurse children. But there is an Indonesian society in which men are expected to be more nurturant and home-oriented than women, because in this society men are viewed as the weaker sex.[3] Anthropologist Mary Catherine Bateson reports that young Iranian men—even when they come to America—are expected to separate from their parents only gradually, and then are expected to take time and energy to care for their aging mothers; they are respected by older males for doing this.[4]

Differential valuing of autonomy and dependence often is reflected in the roles expected of the sexes. When nurturance and relationship are seen primarily as "dependent" activities, they tend to be assigned to female people and tend not to be rewarded with social status and privilege. Activities associated with autonomy and independence then will be assigned to men and associated with greater privilege and status.

Although roles and identities vary widely among societies and cultures, there is one gender difference that seems almost universal in today's world: men have more power than women. This is true even in societies where women are widely educated—in the Scandinavian countries, for example. Differences in power and social roles play an important part in self-esteem and perhaps in mental health, although power difference rarely is included in our interpretation of mental health.[5] When power is defined as decision making, status, and control of resources, whether at home or in the workplace, it becomes clear that power affects the ways we feel about ourselves and others.

This becomes significant psychologically when we recognize that a major component of gender difference worldwide is power difference, with female people having less power. Some of this power difference is economic. Most national economic systems depend upon women's unpaid or underpaid labor in order to function.[6] If women suddenly were paid equitably for the work they do, economic stability probably would collapse everywhere. No wonder the fight for equal rights for women feels so threatening—it threatens the world's economy as it now exists. This fact is all the more significant because women now constitute 52 percent (a majority) of the world's population.[7] There are many reasons, both conscious and unconscious, that people become anxious about gender, especially in its connection to power.

As a strong organizer of our interpersonal world, gender powerfully controls meaning. Most of us feel compelled to get gender established quickly, both at the birth of a child and in any social situation.[8] If an infant's sex is anomalous at birth, the elders organize quickly to assign a gender and change the body of the infant to approximate as closely as possible that of the associated sex.

Many adults find the gender-neutral clothes of some of today's teenagers anxiety-provoking, uncomfortable, or even perverse. "What *is* this person's sex?" We feel compelled to answer that question whenever we encounter someone new. As with the anomalous infant, we cannot take a wait-and-see attitude or be open to any other categories than masculine and feminine. Gender opens the way to fantasy, symbol, and language. How can I engage with a person unless I feel certain about assigning the category that will determine so much of what I expect and perceive?

There are many conscious and unconscious consequences of the division of the human community into two genders. The depth-psychological themes surrounding sex and gender rarely have been treated sensitively and adequately in any school of psychoanalysis. Typically these themes have been tied to essentialist or biological arguments that women and men are "born this way." This leads to psychological theories about what is missing, left out, or diminished in one or the other sex.

Since most of the major theorists of psychoanalysis have been androcentric, taking male people to be the standard of health and competence, most of their theories have described female people in terms of what they lack: a penis, the phallus, power, objectivity, intelligence, moral fiber, or cultural strivings.[9] Such theories then assume that females, because of what they lack, "naturally" are depressed, masochistic, or narcissistic.

Responding to such inadequate accounts of male-female difference, and embracing the idea of gender as narrative or construct, Freudian psychoanalyst Roy Schafer provides a strong corrective for Freud's errors, when Schafer writes: "We must conclude that Freud's estimates of women's morality and objectivity are logically and empirically indefensible. In large part these estimates implement conventional patriarchal values and judgments that have been misconstrued as being disinterested, culture-free scientific observations."[10]

Jung, too, believed that men and women fulfilled different biological and social destinies.[11] Because male and female people were assumed to be shaped by archetypes of Masculinity and Femininity, each sex was thought to embody the complementary opposite of the other. As I said earlier, the Masculine was characterized as Logos, independence, culture, and objectivity; whereas the Feminine was Eros, dependence, nature, and subjectivity. Jung's estimates of male and female character have also demanded correction by a clearheaded, empirically-based review of the attributes and differences of sex and gender. Several Jungian analysts and theorists have written such correctives: Demaris Wehr (1987), Polly Young-Eisendrath and Florence Wiedemann (1987), Mary Ann Mattoon and Jennifer Jones (1987), Andrew Samuels (1989), Claire Douglas (1990), Deldon McNeely (1991), and again Polly Young-Eisendrath (1993).[12] Even with this kind of critical concern about, and revision of, Jungian concepts, much theorizing that sounds like naïve realism continues to refer to the Feminine and the Masculine as if they were categories inherent in things and people themselves.

Many psychoanalytic theories that account for sex and gender differences confound the two, assuming that sex differences undergird "natural" gendered behaviors. Most psychodynamic theorizing about gender has been deeply flawed by reducing gender to sex and accounting for sex differences in terms of social stereotypes. These stereotypes—for example, the view that women are less logical (more subjective in their thinking) and men are more

logical (more objective)—generally are supported by realist explanations indicating that somehow we were "born that way."[13]

Jung's psychology in some ways is an exception to this tendency to stereotype. With his idea of contrasexuality, the notion
that each of us has an unconscious (or less conscious) personality
of the opposite sex, Jung has added complexity to our concept of
two genders. He calls our attention to a central aspect in the psychology of gender: the opposite sex as a projection-making factor.
In his theories of anima and animus, Jung awakens us to the reality that we see aspects of ourselves in our images of the opposite
sex, especially when we idealize or devalue those others.[14]

Jung's theory of anima and animus (the Latin names he gave to
the contrasexual personalities of men and women, respectively) is
both a cultural analysis of universal opposites and a psychology of
projection. Expressed as emotionally laden archetypal images
which often are projected into people of the opposite sex, these
contrasexual subpersonalities develop over a lifetime and come
into play in a new way in midlife or after the reproductive period
has ended. In midlife or later, we tend to question our earlier com-
mitments and may begin to recognize the Other within and desire
to realize its potential. Jung's theory of contrasexuality is a contribution to depth psychology that problematizes our stereotypes
about the "opposite sex," tracing the shadow of Otherness back to
its owner. In contrast to Freud's more narrowly focused biological
theories of gender, Jung's theory of contrasexuality seems fluid and
broadly useful, in a postmodern world where we recognize that our
own subjectivity may color much of what we perceive as outside
ourselves.[15]

On the other hand, the theory of contrasexuality, as it originally was cast by Jung, *is* colored by essentialism. Although he
wavered on whether anima and animus were archetypes or
complexes, he often thought of them as archetypes. Thus, our contrasexuality was to be understood as a biologically based subpersonality derived from genetic, hormonal, and morphological

traces of the opposite sex. Described this way, these opposite archetypes have the universal attributes of the Feminine (anima)
and the Masculine (animus). Accordingly, every man's anima
would have certain universal qualities, as would every woman's animus. Personalities of the two sexes, both conscious and unconscious, then tend to be preconceived and typed, and all the
mystery of the relationship between self and Other tends to
disappear.

Making a strong and complementary division between these
opposites almost eliminates their psychological usefulness. Anima
and animus are useful in helping us understand ourselves if they
encompass a range of Otherness—what we feel is absent in ourselves and dreaded or desired in others: the positive or negative potential that is projected onto the opposite sex. As Jacqueline Rose
says in her introduction to the English translation of Jacques Lacan's *Feminine Sexuality*:

> Sexuality belongs in this area of instability played out in the register of
> demand and desire, each sex coming to stand . . . for that which could
> satisfy and complete the other. It is when the categories "male" and
> "female" are seen to represent an absolute and complementary divi-
> sion that they fall prey to a mystification in which the difficulty of sex-
> uality instantly disappears.[16]

Seeing the two sexes as inherent complements of each other, with
specific roles assigned to each, eliminates our curiosity and interest in, and sometimes even our desire to know about, the Others—
those unknown aspects of ourselves that we believe exist in the
opposite sex.

Contrasexuality as Strange Gender

In my own practice and theorizing of contrasexuality, I have revised the concepts of anima and animus, concepts that I find extremely valuable in a nonessentialist approach to psychotherapy
with individuals and couples.[17] A feminist analysis of gender has

provided a framework within which Jung's theory of contrasexuality illuminates the issues of desire, projection, projective identification, and opposites, especially between the sexes.

Feminist studies and interpretations of gender and sex differences effectively have undermined theories of biological femininity and masculinity. From all available empirical studies of sex and gender differences, it appears that *no* long-standing personality traits—such as initiative-taking, dependence, intelligence, or even aggression—are consistently different between the sexes over a lifetime.[18] Instead, it appears that gender differences are culturally constructed roles, identities, and categories that permit societies to assign men and women to different tasks and potentials. From many of the same studies, we have discovered that male and female people have strong expectations of each other—expectations that the others will fit into certain roles and patterns; and that, when people of opposite sexes are in direct relationship, they will think and act in accord with some of the stereotyped beliefs that they have been socialized to hold true of the two sexes.[19]

When scientists or others want to demonstrate that sex differences create predictable gender differences, they start from premises and ask questions different from those assumed or asked by people who want to know whether or not sex differences exist at the level of personality and psychological functioning. Biological explanations of gender, based on studies of hormonal and brain chemistry, for example, *begin* with the assumption that predictable differences between the sexes exist; then the studies seek to explain these differences. In scientific studies, as in other kinds of studies, the premises and assumptions of the researchers create biases. Only through the recent influence of feminism, which has no unified platform or premise regarding gender differences, have gender studies opened up to include the question, "Are there really lasting differences between the sexes?" Previously, psychologists had assumed that sex differences were realities, although most psychological studies were done exclusively on men and then generalized to women.[20]

In the past twenty years or so, feminism has informed gender research in such a way as to generate new questions that have allowed us to see a new reality. Most psychological researchers of gender now would say that healthy men and women should have available to them a wide range of potentials for acting and defining themselves in relation to their bodies, gender, and identities, and that gender identities shift over the lifespan. Increasingly, with the breakdown of gender stereotyping, this attitude is described more often in terms of realizing full human potential, rather than specifically developing "androgyny." The latter concept is still premised upon categories of feminine and masculine.

Analytical psychology is strengthened as we clarify the flexibility of gender and recognize that the constraints of being born into a male or female body take on different meanings in different contexts. I would agree with my Freudian colleague, Roy Schafer (1992), who has written on some of these same issues in relation to Freudian psychoanalysis, that "logically, there is no right answer to the questions of what is masculine and what is feminine and what is active and what is passive. There are no preconceptual facts to be discovered and arrayed. There are only loose conventions governing the uses and groupings of the words in question."[21] Rather than assign specific meaning to these categories, we can discover the meaning that female and male people bring to them in psychotherapy or elsewhere. How, for instance, does a young American man of Puerto-Rican background define his masculinity, in contrast to the way a middle-aged Jewish-American man does? What would an older woman returning to college after raising four children say about being "feminine"? How would a nineteen-year-old lesbian college student address the same issue? I assume that whatever an individual identifies as "feminine" or "masculine" should be accepted as a starting point from which to examine the psychological meanings of identity. Similarly, gender confusion, when presented by an individual either consciously or unconsciously, should be accepted as confusion, even if the person appears to fulfill the requirements of one or another gender category, according to conventional gender stereotypes.

This does not mean that I ignore the broad cultural definitions of gender identity, especially in relation to particular age cohorts. In fact, I always keep in mind the general cultural context of gender: female sexual identity will look different to a nineteen-year-old college student than it will to a forty-six-year-old working mother. If I meet a nineteen-year-old who sounds more like a forty-six-year-old, I am curious. In other words, I use conventional categories about what is considered "normal" within a particular context, but I also keep my categories fluid and open.

In this regard, in my own clinical experience (which is not a fair sample of what is in the world), I have noticed that generally young men who come for therapy are more anxious about their gender—what it means to be male—than are older men or women of any age who see me in therapy. Although we could understand this unease in terms of "castration anxiety" about being required to prove themselves in a patriarchal world, I have found that these young men feel confused because of current cultural changes. They long for some clarity, the clarity they imagine existed in the past (the 1950s, for example) concerning what it means to be a man (and a woman). When we look more deeply into their confusion, often we find that these men are afraid to claim as "masculine" what they take to be fundamental in themselves. For instance, if a man has more tender, romantic feelings about family life than he has competitive desires for work life, he may feel that he is "too wimpy." Through psychotherapy, he may come to accept his gender identity as male and masculine simply because it belongs to him, a male being. Perhaps he identified more with Mother than Father in growing up. Does this make him more feminine? If a man is homosexual, with some of the gender traits typically considered "bitchy" in the homosexual world, are these

"feminine traits," or are they "masculine," since they have been
devised and developed by men?

When we allow people to explore the meaning of self-
identified gender, we begin to see what is left out, what is considered to be Other. The character of the subjective Other, the anima
or animus, then emerges. In Jungian terms, this is contrasexuality
as a psychological complex rather than as an archetype.

An earlier section described Jung's later theory of a psychological complex as a cluster of associations around an archetypal core
of emotional arousal, uniting the personal and the collective unconscious. In regard to contrasexuality, I assume that the core archetype is Other (not-self), constellating not only the anima or
animus, but other alien complexes as well, such as Shadow and
Negative Parent. In the case of gender, this archetype of Other has
a powerful effect in organizing a subpersonality of meaning and
identity, because it is experienced as Opposite. Any image I see as
my own sex or gender potentially could be part of me, but that
which I see as my opposite is going to be alien.

In this theory of animus or anima as contrasexual complex, my
assumption is that everyone identifies with some gendered characteristics, feelings, and attitudes as a conscious self. As this conscious personality develops from its earliest images and fantasies of
gender, body, and self, there also develops an unconscious complementary aspect of Otherness, a subpersonality of the opposite
sex, based on images and fantasies of that opposite sex. Naturally,
this contrasexual complex contains both idealized and devalued
aspects of the personality which cannot be tolerated in conscious
awareness and must be relegated to Other. For instance, if I identify myself as pleasing and nice, then I tend not to see myself as irritating and mean; in conflicts with others, I tend to see *them* as
irritating and mean. If these latter qualities are conceived as truly
"opposite" of me, they can be assigned to the opposite sex, to be
elaborated as fears and fantasies about those others.

I call this contrasexual complex our "strange gender."[22] It takes on specific meaning in childhood, when we come to realize that the two sexes belong to mutually exclusive clubs—that we can belong to one only and must view the other as composed of strangers. With this realization, our strange gender begins to be transformed into specific images of what I call "dream lovers"—those subjective Others whom we fear and desire because we imagine that they are different from us.

Although children begin to think in gender categories almost as soon as they can identify a separate embodied self, around eighteen months of age, they do not understand the permanence and exclusivity of this concept until much later.[23] Very young children easily may say, for instance, that boys have penises and girls do not, or that boys run faster than girls; but they do not grasp the power of this difference—that it permanently may constrain who they themselves can become. Nor do they understand that sex cannot be changed through changing one's appearance or name, or that some of these exclusive differences will last a lifetime. Quite a few three-, four-, or five-year-olds will change names, hairstyles, dress styles, and other things to try to change into the opposite sex.

Only with entry into elementary school and with the mental maturity of six or seven years, when practical reasoning (Piaget's term) begins to develop, will a child be able to grasp the exclusive nature of gender. This is called "gender conservation." I will be a *girl forever*. You will be a *boy forever*. No matter what clothes I wear, how I cut my hair, how fast I run, what toys I play with, I am stuck in this body and this club. The meaning of sex and gender gradually becomes clearer, and children begin to feel directly how limited they are by embodiment and how this limitation stretches into the future.

At the point of gender conservation, many children rebel. They are bold in their protests: "What do you *mean* that I can't have a baby? Why not? You did it, Mommy!" "*Why* can't I play with the boys? My brother does it all the time!" From this moment on, strange gender will have a major influence on development.

We will feel "driven" by fantasies of freedom and desire that we project onto the opposite sex. The rights and privileges of the opposite sex may seem profoundly unfair, because they seem to come about simply from embodiment, from having been born that way.

Young children, even prior to school age, discover that characteristics of maleness and masculinity are associated with strength and freedom, while characteristics of femaleness and femininity are associated more with niceness and passivity. No matter how much parents strive to keep things equal between the sexes among their children, everyone eventually gets the message (implied or direct) that boys somehow are more important or better than girls. Young girls, if they choose, often are permitted to play and look like boys without a lot of social condemnation.[24] Young girls can try out their animus preferences as tomboys, at least until they become teenagers. Young boys, on the other hand, are not permitted to play and look like girls without social condemnation. They are forbidden to act out their anima fantasies. A powerful message is implied in this fundamental cultural display: there is something wrong with being a girl, because no boy should want to be one.[25]

Over the childhood years, our ideas about the strange gender are discussed mostly among our same-sex peers. Until late adolescence, girls and boys tend to segregate into same-sex groups for play and relationships.[26] They share confidences and make up stories about those Others. Our families shape our original gender complexes of self and other, especially through the unconscious meanings associated with mother or father or sister or brother; but our peers and the media initiate us into stories about the Others, about their sexuality and desire and powers.

By the time we arrive at young adulthood, we will have many ideals and fears about the other sex, and most will be based less upon actual friendships than upon fantasies. This mix of gossip, allusion, illusion, and story about the opposite sex will shape our personalities in important ways.

Sex, Envy, Equality

When people maintain a rigid gender identity, based strongly upon the roles culturally sanctioned for male and female people, they risk losing parts of themselves forever. In other words, if you believe that your gender is based entirely upon your sex, you will assume that a wide range of possibilities belong exclusively to the opposite sex. You will have strong responses to this half-life, and you will externalize or project your contrasexuality. Instead of recognizing it in yourself, you will encounter it through projection, envy, and idealization. This was the situation typical in the traditional heterosexual couple until about twenty years ago, when other possibilities began to open up. Many men and women in traditional, gender-segregated marriages suffered from depression, because so many possibilities were unavailable—for men, the traditionally "feminine" potentials of tenderness, dependence, relatedness; and for women, the traditionally "masculine" potentials of strength, autonomy, authority.

But even in the contemporary world, with its much greater gender flexibility, women and men still are constrained by their gender and their embodiment. These constraints lead to envy and idealization of the opposite sex. Although some constraints are biological and others are social, our concern is with the *meaning* connected to the constraints and not the constraints *per se*.

Psychoanalyst Melanie Klein has developed a useful distinction between envy and jealousy.[27] In her framework, *envy* is the desire to destroy what another has, because one cannot possess it for oneself. Envy is a form of hatred. It is a belittling, or emptying out, of the value, meaning, and potential of another, because one feels that one cannot possess certain resources the other has. Many murders are committed in a state of envy. It is a very destructive emotion.

Jealousy, on the other hand, is the desire to possess what another has. In jealousy, one feels the capability or possibility of getting what another has. Jealousy can lead to competition, initiative-taking, and developing something new; but envy cannot.

Envy usually is unconscious, although sometimes it is conscious and may be rationalized or reduced through humor. In regard to the opposite sex, envy most often is expressed by belittling and trivializing the other's resources, capacities, or desires. We all have heard men belittle women for being too emotional and irrational. And we have heard women belittle men for being relationally incompetent. Envy between the sexes is handled mostly with humor or frustration, but sometimes the hatred is so strong that the other person is dreaded. In such a case, the other is seen (through projection) as empty of resources and then dreaded; you assume that the other will annihilate you to "even the score."

Women and men often envy the biological potentials of their opposites. Whereas women may envy the physical strength (and the freedom accompanying it) that they see in men, men may envy the ability to give birth (and engage in the relational possibilities accompanying it) that they see in women. There are many forms of fantasied reproductive envy—penis, testicles, breast, womb, vagina—but envy between the sexes is not confined to reproductive issues. Women tend to see doctors for physical complaints approximately six times more often than men do during the midlife years.[28] They envy men's apparently less complicated health picture. On the other hand, women, on the average, across many different societies and cultures, outlive men by approximately eight years. Men envy women's greater longevity.

The flip side of envy is idealization. This is a way of seeing the other as full of resources and potentials, psychic and other qualities and supplies, that one would like to have in one's own possession, under one's control. Biological differences between the sexes can lead to idealization. Look at the cultural institution of motherhood; although actual mothers have little prestige or status, the idealization of motherhood leads us to speak of it in hushed tones.[29]

Envy plays itself out in gender as well as sex differences. Gender is more flexible than biology, but we look around and see certain privileges that the opposite sex appears to have, simply because of biology. This seems unfair. We want to protest, but instead we belittle what the others have. Often women envy men's greater freedom in the world and their ability to earn more money. Men's earnings then are taken for granted or trivialized in comparison with women's relational skills in the family. Men often envy what they take to be women's lesser responsibilities for wage earning and greater involvement with children, relatives, and friends. What happens? Men put women down for being unable to earn a living and also fail to appreciate the skills and capacities involved in keeping alive and intact a family and a network of friendships.

With envy, jealousy, and competition operating in regard to the opposite sex, we find some strong, primitive emotions and images in our strange gender—played out in many heterosexual couples. In falling in love and in battling one's partner, when a dream lover is activated, people may experience powerful emotions (including hatred) that they rarely feel elsewhere in their adult lives. Sometimes, when people come for couples therapy, they say that they have such negative feelings for each other—distinctly more negative than for others in their lives—that they believe they should split up. These feelings seem symptomatic of loss of love. My response is that there is *no* other relationship, except perhaps with one's children and parents, in which one is likely to experience such powerful drives, fantasies, and ideals. In projecting one's contrasexuality into one's partner, and in trying to control it by controlling the partner, one will encounter some of the darkest and most exciting aspects of the psyche.

In examining Jung's original theory of anima and animus, I now bring to bear my clinical experience of almost fifteen years of doing couples therapy, using a model called Dialogue Therapy that my husband and I originated. Dialogue Therapy is a Jungian approach that allows us to unpack the unconscious projections and identifications between partners.[30] Couples sometimes present a level and intensity of hatred, fear, and threat that I rarely see in individual or group psychotherapy. From these experiences, I have gained greater sympathy for Jung's original manner of theorizing the anima and animus.

Even my first encounters with Jung's theory of anima and animus worried me, because I found his categories to be sexist; and that was before I knew much about sexism. I could see that his theory was hampered by certain idealizations of "femininity" and some bitterness (envy, perhaps?) toward women. Later I came to see that Jung's categories of Masculine and Feminine were not archetypes but were based upon cultural conventions. I found that I could separate out the theory of anima and animus as "contrasexual complexes"—cohering around the archetype of Other—and be freed of the problems of sexism that burdened the original theory. But always I felt quite critical of Jung's descriptions of anima and animus, believing that, in his observations of men and women, he had been misled by his own personal dynamics and shortcomings. I found his descriptions unconvincing, even insulting to women, in part because I could not step into his shoes and see what the world was like in his day.

Seeing now the role played by envy and idealization between the sexes, I also can see why Jung[31] thought contrasexuality was rooted in archetypes of Masculine and Feminine, in primitive emotional states of opposites. He thought anima and animus had to be archetypes, filled with particular content, because they often were linked to the raw energy that epitomizes an archetype. We now can see that the primitive emotions associated with contrasexuality are based upon the *division* of the human community into two realms, two subjectivities. This division encourages splitting, idealization, envy, fear, and fantasy—the kinds of emotions that Jung probably witnessed in regard to the categories traditional for the sexes of his day.

When Jung wrote about the anima, he often sounded as if he were caught up in an idealization of the content, the stuff of anima. Here is one passage that he wrote about this male "projection-making factor" in 1951:

> Every mother and every beloved is forced to become the carrier and embodiment of this omnipresent and ageless image, which corresponds to the deepest reality in a man. It belongs to him, this perilous image of Woman; she stands for the loyalty which in the interests of life he must sometimes forgo; she is the much needed compensation for the risks, struggles, sacrifices that all end in disappointment; she is the solace for all the bitterness of life.[32]

And he says further that she "possesses all the outstanding characteristics of a feminine being." This kind of idealization naturally would lead to problems, if men felt they could be manipulated by women who captured or controlled the anima.

What I can see more clearly now is that Jung's descriptions of anima were based upon what he witnessed clinically and felt in his own experience in a heavily sex-typed culture such as Jung's Switzerland was (and is). Jung had few opportunities to witness what the anima might be like in a man who comfortably had shifted some of his gender roles—being, for example, involved in vital child care for young children and infants—and so did not feel deeply excluded from female roles.

Jung's comparable account of a woman's animus is hardly idealizing. Here he must have observed women's envious and hostile responses to male privilege. Swiss women of his day must have felt bitterly constrained by the limitations of roles. For Jung, the masculinity of women was not so exotic as the femininity of men:

> I have called the projection-making factor in women the animus, which means mind or spirit. The animus corresponds to the paternal Logos just as the anima corresponds to the maternal Eros . . . In women . . . Eros is an expression of their true nature, while their Logos is often only a regrettable accident. It gives rise to misundertand-

ings and annoying interpretations in the family circle and among friends. This is because it consists of opinions instead of reflections, and by opinions I mean a priori assumptions that lay claim to absolute truth . . . No matter how friendly and obliging a woman's Eros may be, no logic on earth can shake her if she is ridden by the animus. Often the man has the feeling and he is not altogether wrong that only seduction or a beating or rape would have the necessary power of persuasion.[33]

Obviously this is a very sexist, even misogynist, passage, and perhaps is based in part on Jung's envy of women. Let us give him the benefit of the doubt, though, and imagine what it might have been like to be a woman in Switzerland before getting the vote, before being allowed education.

Here were women well into the twentieth century, in a highly developed culture, without personal sovereignty. Their lack of privileges was based entirely on their sex. How women must have envied men's greater privileges in education, leadership, and personal freedom. They must have felt, consciously or unconsciously, compelled to argue forcefully, especially when they were denied access to education and information available to their male counterparts.

In other words, perhaps the sexual inequality of Switzerland in the 1940s and 1950s intensified idealization and envy of the opposite sex. These deep and powerfully emotional experiences then were factored into theories of biological differences between the sexes. Conflating sex and gender, such theories could only have intensified opposition, idealization, and envy between the sexes. Perhaps Jung was fairly objective in his account of what he witnessed in the unconscious dynamics of contrasexuality.

Unfortunately, in this area of his theorizing, he was a naive realist. He simply reported what he saw, believing it based in biology, not culture. Nor was Jung an exception in this; rather, this kind of realism was the rule. Where Jung was exceptional was in holding strongly to a theory of contrasexuality; Freud, whose theory of bisexuality might have saved him from reducing the sexes to stereotypes, tended over time to drop his notion of bisexuality. In seeing the potential for development, in both oneself and others, to be derived from withdrawing contrasexual projections and claiming them as part of the self, Jung was far ahead of his time. But because he divided the world into complementary sexes, he lost sight of the mystery of how the two sexes interact within an array of differences and similarities.

At the end of the twentieth century, analytical psychology is well positioned to open up Jung's theory of contrasexuality to include this lost mystery. Finally we can understand our contrasexuality as a fluid and changing complex of what we may see as the opposite sex. Finally we can understand more fully how the archetype of opposite can be used for defensive splitting and idealization.

Gender Narratives and the Postmodern Self

Although we certainly do not yet understand fully the impact of gender on the development of identity, we have some understanding of the role of narrative—of the story that is told about gender in the development of self. Recently I was asked by a friend what, based on my own experience and my reviews of the literature on gender difference, I thought was the "most important gender difference" between male and female people.

I thought for only a moment and replied that, in our society, a major gender difference that has lifelong impact is the expectation of achievement.[34] From many studies, we know that boys, especially in adolescence, tend to overestimate their potential. Whether in academics or athletics, adolescent boys (including young men in college), expect that they will be more successful than they actually will be.

Girls, on the other hand, tend to underestimate their abilities.

Even girls who do extremely well in difficult subjects in school (such as math or science) attribute their performance more to luck than to skill. In terms of self-esteem, girls start elementary school on an equal footing with boys but lose ground as they move through school. A nationwide poll showed that girls' self-esteem declines precipitously in middle school and continues to plummet in high school.[35] Although boys also decline in level of self-esteem over their school years, their drop is not as marked, and it never falls as low as that of girls.

Some of these differences have been attributed to preferential treatment given to male students from elementary school through college. Teachers (both male and female) recall male students' names more often, call on them much more frequently, listen to and critique them more seriously, and respond to their assertive behavior more positively.[36]

A majority of adolescent girls tends to sacrifice academic or athletic achievement for the sake of popularity. Personal appearance and popularity are the resources most valued for middle-school girls, whereas boys at that age take pride in success in both athletics and academics, although they may feel better about athletic success. One psychologist found that the girls with the poorest body-images and most depressive symptoms in the seventh grade were those most academically successful.[37] A year later, the researcher returned, asked the same questions, and discovered that some girls had improved. Those who reported improvements in self-image and in depression were those who had lowered their academic achievement!

Psychologist Carol Gilligan has written extensively about how girls lose their strong spirits and their voices as they enter adolescence.[38] She attributes this loss to girls' needs for close relationships, honesty, and connection, needs demeaned and trivialized in a patriarchal society. Girls surrender their own perspectives and accept traditional "feminine values," in order to avoid losing close relationships, since such losses would lead to a loss of self, according to Gilligan. She suspects that loss of spirit and voice in adolescent girls accounts for the rise in depression and the drop in achievement so characteristic of many girls in middle school and high school.

These fundamental differences in self-estimation—male overestimating and female underestimating—have many implications in adult life. This difference may account for the greater depression reported and assessed among adult women.[39] It may account for differences in how men and women present themselves in conversation, and how they draw conclusions about what they know and who they are.

I have found the difference in male and female self-estimation to be surprisingly important in the time of midlife, when identity shifts. My observations underscore the importance of Jung's theory of midlife identity crisis. In midlife, people of both sexes often are influenced by contrasexuality, especially in seeing members of the opposite sex in envious and competitive, or idealizing and erotic, ways. A curious reversal of feelings about oneself may emerge. Women, as they examine their lives more closely and look either at what they have achieved or at what they intend now to achieve, often feel pleased with themselves.[40] After all, a woman who thought she would never achieve anything at all will be extremely pleased to have gotten good grades as a returning student, may be overjoyed to discover that her small business has been chosen for an award, or may see her contributions to a helping profession bearing fruit that she had not anticipated. At around the same time, a man who thought he would rise to at least a minor level of leadership in his work will be disappointed to find that his contributions are consistently ordinary. Another who felt he was extremely powerful as a young man (in terms of athletic prowess, for instance) may feel that he has lost all that he ever had and that he has nothing to replace it. A man who has done very well in his business may feel that he has not excelled (in status or accomplishments) in any way that measures up to his adolescent fantasies.

In both women and men, the youthful persona often breaks down in midlife, but emotionally the experience can differ markedly for the two sexes. For a woman, her earlier persona of "plain old me" or "little know-nothing" or "pretty but stupid" no longer feels adequate, and she begins to see how she was duped into taking it on in the first place. For a man, his earlier persona of "great guy" or "Mr. Big" or "always in control" no longer feels right, but he may begin to feel that his life is a failure and believe that he never was as good as he thought. Whatever other idiosyncratic fantasies may be supporting these gendered personas, there have been some cultural and social supports for them, too. This aspect of gender narrative—self-estimation of achievements—is but one of the cultural themes typical of differences between the sexes.

Gendered stories of who we are and what we should become surround us daily.[41] They are inescapable, but we can become conscious of how they affect us. We can begin to examine the splits within ourselves, the ways in which our identities may be constrained unnecessarily or our prejudices about the opposite sex may be unnecessarily defensive. In order to do this, we also need to revise the ways in which we think about the self, from both a personal and a theoretical viewpoint.

Jung's post-1944 theory of self focused upon an ego complex at the core of which is the archetype of Self.[42] Our ordinary experience of being an individual—a separate subject of our own thoughts, desires, and actions—has formed as the result of an inherent predisposition for unity or wholeness. As noted earlier, the unification of the personal and collective unconscious in the concept of a psychological complex (with an archetypal core), moved Jung's theory beyond the limitations of realism. Defining the archetype as a predisposition to form an image, an innate tendency for an image to cohere in an emotionally aroused state, Jung no longer pointed to a realm or dimension beyond human experience. The archetype arises through embodiment as a human being, as part of the structure of this form of life.

Postmodernism and feminism, in many forms, have been powerfully critical of the bounded, individual self—that account of subjectivity that has been fostered by stories of a strong, independent individual who conquers inner or outer landscapes alone.[43]

The archetype of Self, as a predisposition to form a unitary image and to integrate the personality around this core, is a *problematizing* of an individual self. It opens up and elaborates the belief that the personality, human subjectivity, is not naturally unified. There is a strong tendency to fall apart, to divide into multiples, to decenter; but there is a counteracting tendency to bring coherence to this disunity again and again throughout the lifespan.

Jung conceived of the natural, unconscious personality as a loose association of multiple psychological complexes, the most conscious being the ego complex.[44] Both at birth and throughout the lifespan, the development of unity is a problem that is never solved. The experiences of the individual will either support or undermine such an integration. At first the integration is unconscious, grounded in adequate caregiving, including the psychological functions of mirroring and empathy. It results in a coherent location in a body, a sense of psyche-body unity, and a continuity over time—the capacity to have memories of self.

Later, if an individual is psychologically healthy, the integration becomes conscious through the ego complex and eventually includes the possibility of self-reflection on its development, the ability to analyze its parts and recognize unconscious motivations and tendencies. What Jung called "individuation" actually was this final step: the capacity for insight into one's unconscious motivations, coming as the byproduct of neurotic breakdown of the persona.

I believe that this theory of subjectivity—of an ego complex with an archetypal core—is remarkably consonant with contemporary constructivism and is especially useful on a clinical and experiential basis. One's shift of awareness from an original "ego" perspective to a later and more comprehensive Self perspective is a process of decentering. The "I" of subjectivity moves from its identity with a separate defended ego to an awareness of a different kind of center, located between the ego and other complexes; this center seems to hold the whole together. One does not identify oneself with the Self archetype, but one senses its presence. Although many postmodern theorists of psychoanalysis theorize multiple selves and multiple centers, they also have to account for the experience of unity, and this they often fail to do adequately.

Jung's account is both elegant and simple: the potential exists for greater and greater unity through consciousness and the development of *integrity*, or spiritual wholeness.[45] Of course, consciousness is dependent upon many relational and cultural factors. Let us examine some important aspects of the postmodern self and then look at its interface with analytical psychology.

Until fairly recently, it was radical or even provocative to critique the individual self of personal autonomy—the bounded self of individual heroism and genius. When such critiques appeared in the 1980s, they tended to be seen as outsider views; but now, in the second half of the 1990s, they have become insider views. We seem to have come into a new *Zeitgeist*, in which many theorists, in psychology, philosophy, theology, and literature, claim that the self is originally and continually the product of a relational matrix and thus is neither free nor independent.[46] They also claim that we find many different versions of self in different cultures and that some of these are more individual and others more collective. Therefore we cannot talk about a universal development toward a more and more autonomous, individual self. Instead, we have to talk about an array of different kinds of selves that develop in relationship to their own cultures and families, selves more or less autonomous, more or less relational, and so on, according to context. Postmodern theories have arisen, then, in response to these critiques.

The premises of such theories in response to critiques made by feminists, philosophers, anthropologists, and developmental researchers (such as infant researchers) generally are: (1) selves are created and developed in relationships, not within the individual; (2) the geography (boundaries and domain) of selves carries the meanings and nuances of families, gender, class, and ethnicity, in ways that cannot be reduced to a formula; and (3) healthy selves may be more or less bounded, more or less collective, more or less unique, depending upon the cultural context in which they were developed.

Several philosophers have contributed significantly to clarifying these premises. Among them are Rom Harré, John Mac-Murray, P. F. Strawson, and Charles Taylor.[47] From their work especially, I gradually have come to understand the self as a set of attitudes, beliefs, images, and actions that permits a person to sustain the sense of being an individual subject, of operating as a separate center of action.

These philosophers distinguish between two concepts of subjectivity: person and self. *Person* refers to public criteria, such as bodily form and capacities, that seem obvious; we never would confuse a person and a corpse, for example. *Self* refers to a set of beliefs—something that is not public and which depends upon an interpretive context or community.

If you encounter a person from another culture, a distant part of the world, you will surely expect certain things—ways of moving (upright), some capacity to be a subject, some kind of language, and so on. You would not confuse a person with an animal or a statue, for instance. You may be able to interact with such a person in emotional exchanges, in protocommunication. But you would have great difficulty knowing anything about this person's *self* without knowing the culture and community from which the person comes. The self is a personal or private set of beliefs.

All people everywhere develop selves, and all those selves are gendered, as I have said earlier. Gender, like other aspects of the self, is a set of beliefs that derives from stories, fantasies, identities, and so on, that are considered important by the family and the community. As the body matures, one amasses both bodily and social experiences that are laden with emotion. One imagines a great deal about oneself and others.

So far, then, I have been tracing the specific emphasis on relationship, narrative, and multiple meanings that postmodernism has contributed to self theories. Jung's concept of an ego complex is resonant with the definition of self as a set of attitudes, beliefs, images, and actions that permits a person to sustain the experience of being an individual.

But what about the archetype of Self? How can we describe Jung's idea of Self without falling into the dual traps of essentialism and realism, without sounding as if we have stepped outside the human arena and know what is really real?

Buddhist No-Self

For my part, I have found it useful to meld Jung's later understanding of the Self as an empty center with a Buddhist analysis of no-self. Jung was quite interested in, and, late in his life, convinced of the value of, Buddhism. According to the religious scholar Huston Smith, "The book C. G. Jung was reading on his deathbed was Charles Luk's *Ch'an and Zen Teachings: First Series*, and he expressly asked his secretary to write to tell the author that 'he was enthusiastic . . . When he read what Hsu Yun said, he sometimes felt as if he himself could have said exactly this.'"[48] Jung himself wrote in 1939, in his foreword to D. T. Suzuki's *Introduction to Zen Buddhism*, of the comparable goals of psychotherapy and Zen meditation:

> *Psychotherapy is at bottom a dialectical relationship between a doctor and patient. It is an encounter, a discussion between two psychic wholes, in which knowledge is used only as a tool. The goal is transformation — not one that is predetermined, but rather an indeterminable change, the only criterion of which is the disappearance of egohood. No efforts on the part of the doctor can compel this experience. The most he can do is to smooth the path for the patient and help*

him to attain an attitude which offers the least resistance to the decisive experience.[49]

Given this, I feel justified in expanding some of Jung's later terms regarding the Self through my knowledge of Buddhism.

I believe it was Jung's own intention to present his concept of Self as a universal predisposition to form a unified image of individual subjectivity. This predisposition arises out of a transcendent coherence, that unity of life that is not personal and may be called God, Tao, Buddha Nature, a central organizing principle (of the universe), or other names. Although Jung wavered and contradicted himself, his later concept of Self cannot easily be equated with the Judeo-Christian concept of God. Jung's earliest account of Self as an eternal *imago* or personality—something like the Atman of Hinduism—is resonant with the Judeo-Christian God, but not his later image of an empty center that cannot be grasped through any conventional knowledge. I use Buddhism to illuminate the shift in Jung's theory of Self from imago to empty center, from Atman to *anatman*, or no-self.[50] I believe this is both practical and consistent with the conclusions that Jung appeared to reach in his later years.

Buddhism, like much postmodernism, is a critique of metaphysical theories. The Buddha's original teachings analyze and break down metaphysics without offering anything to replace it. Instead, the Buddha offers a practical method that leads people to their own experience of the transcendent, something that, because of the limitations of our symbolic forms, cannot be captured in any conventional knowledge.

Buddhism denies the existence of a soul or Atman—the latter being the Sanskrit word for the idea propounded by the Brahmans of ancient India during the Buddha's lifetime (about 2,560 years ago).[51] The Brahmans taught that there was a fundamental unchanging or eternal self that was identical with the ultimate Reality of the universe. The Buddha, who was called Prince

Shakymuni before his enlightenment, disagreed. He taught that "the idea of self is an imaginary, false belief which has no corresponding reality, and . . . produces harmful thoughts of 'me' and 'mine,' selfish desire, craving, attachment, hatred, ill-will, conceit, pride, egoism and defilements, impurities and problems." Significantly, he said further that "to this false view can be traced all the evil of the world."[52] The teaching and experience of no-self were essential to emancipating human beings from suffering. Such an experience would awaken them to the fundamental fact of existence: interdependence.

When this idea of no-self is translated into Western languages, confusions often arise. Frequently no-self is confused with no-ego or being selfless. From this have ensued many misunderstandings about the psychological problems of having "no ego," or being without boundaries or defenses. After reading many Buddhist accounts of this teaching and its interpretation, it seems to me that the Buddhist no-self means no separate self, no reality in being isolated, cut off, or set apart from other beings. Buddhism does not demean ego functions such as reality testing and taking initiative. These are, in fact, necessary to pursue the practical methods of meditation and living that the Buddha taught.

At the same time, there is a clear awareness in many Buddhist teachings that human beings desire so strongly to feel that something is permanent and enduring in their existence that they will substantialize passing moods and states of being, as I discussed earlier.[53] In order to overcome this tendency, we must become acutely aware of our impermanence, of our constantly changing psyche and world. Ideals of permanence enter into our discourse, whether or not we intend them; they are the products of fear and self-protection.

Even in Buddhism, the discussion of Buddha Nature or Buddha Mind sometimes can be substantialized and made to sound like a permanent, nondualistic state. But, as contemporary Zen scholar Masao Abe puts it, "Not only conditioned, relative things, but also unconditioned, absolute things are understood to be without self, without their own-being. Accordingly, not only samsara, but also nirvana, not only delusion, but also enlightenment, are without own-being. Neither relative nor absolute things are self-existing and independent."[54]

I believe it is useful to develop and extend Jung's theory of Self in a way that corresponds both with Buddhism and with contemporary constructivism. First, we must use the concept of Self in a way that keeps it clearly distinguished from our experience of being a person. We must not confuse the two, because that confusion leads to our substantializing the Self. Second, we see the Self simply as a predisposition to coherence, giving rise to the ego complex and individuation.

The evidence for this is that people everywhere construct a self. They have both the experience and their own "theories" of unitary subjectivity. As philosopher Rom Harré says, "Animate beings are fully human if they are in possession of a theory—a theory about themselves. It is a theory in terms of which a being orders, partitions, and reflects on its own experience and becomes capable of self intervention and control."[55] From the perspective of analytical psychology, the first step of the development of subjectivity is to come fully into possession of an ego complex, a set of beliefs or a theory about oneself as an individual.

This first step depends, of course, upon the adequacy of early relationships and upon the capacity of the individual to unify the multiple perceptions, emotions, cognitions, and actions into an ego complex of continuous body-being. Philosopher Charles Taylor reminds us that individual subjectivity means dependence upon others: "One is a self only among other selves. A self can never be described without reference to those who surround it," says Taylor.[56] If early relationships have been able to support enough of a person's developing self, then other relationships will become the arena for its further development.

If development progresses beyond adolescence and early adulthood, the next step is the breakdown of the *defenses* of the ego complex (persona and shadow), so that one feels oneself to be not unitary but multiple—to have conflicting motivations, desires, and values that arise in a number of different unconscious complexes which cannot be encompassed by the ego. This is the process I mentioned earlier as the "breakdown of the persona"— typically the gendered persona of adolescence that has protected the assumption that one's values and motives are known and understandable. Often this persona first becomes threatened in a committed couple relationship, in which one's desires and needs come into conflict with a partner's. Out of this kind of confrontation, eventually one must feel and acknowledge subpersonalities that are not-I, not ego, if development is to continue. Many people resist such a development and instead spend most of their adult lives defending and rationalizing their unconscious motives and desires.

To develop fully into psychological wholeness or *individuation*, one must move to a new unity—a self-awareness or responsibility for one's multiple selves and motives.[57] One becomes responsible for one's own subjectivity. No longer does one simply project one's negative complexes onto others. No longer does one blame the world or others for one's suffering. No longer does one attempt to control in someone else that which has been externalized or excluded from the self. In this lifelong process and struggle for psychological wholeness, one acknowledges and contains much psychological conflict for the sake of further growth and partnership with others.

In the process of individuation, a person comes to read her or his own history—the complexes of the personality—and to tolerate or accept a range of emotions and images, without necessarily acting upon any of them. This capacity for self-reflection opens the door to compassion, to seeing how one suffers as others do— and finally to a realization of interdependence, another level of unity emerging out of multiplicity.

What I have just described is an account of the Self in analytical psychology that is nonessentialist, that does not posit an eternal or ongoing Self, but rather conceives of the Self as a predisposition to unity and coherence within the context of multiplicity and diversity in inner and outer life. Psychological complexes, as multiple centers within the personality, are multiple subjectivities, while the archetype of Self is a tendency toward ever-increasing integration through the differentiation of psychic life within oneself and between oneself and others. The potential for greater integration is no guarantee that anyone will reach it.

At the most complex and integrated stages, the human being dissolves that sense of being an isolated self and begins to experience directly the no-self, the ways in which one is connected not only to other humans, but to all existence. In such a state, one is freer, in the sense of not being ruled by self-centered desires, not being driven by complexes—ego or otherwise—but one is not more independent. In both Buddhism and psychoanalysis, the goal of development is nonattachment, not in the sense of being uncaring or indifferent, but rather in the sense of not being compelled by one's own complexes to do this or that.

Returning, then, to the place where we began—the division of the human psyche into genders, into opposites—opens the way for a number of developments that can lead from desire to individuation, if a person is able to develop the self-awareness and knowledge that allow the process to continue. Along the way, though, there are many traps, the greatest of which is identifying with, and rigidifying in, a particular ego complex, especially a highly gendered one. Then one risks losing aspects of oneself forever, never being able to know one's own story or to free oneself from defensive self-protection. As we shall see in the discussion of the myth of Pandora, a major trap for both sexes lies in believing in the power of female appearance.

CHAPTER THREE

Pandora and the Object of Desire

In trying to comprehend the meaning of desire, I have been strongly influenced by some of the writings of French psychoanalyst Jacques Lacan, whose work is, in many respects, completely impenetrable for me. But Lacan's ideas have been interpreted and expanded in useful commentaries by a number of other psychoanalysts, and many of these works deal with sexuality and desire.

Lacan's theory conceives of desire as a longing for something already known as pleasurable or gratifying. Desire begins with recognizing the absence of a presence that was stimulating or gratifying or comforting. Desire holds within it the sense that something is missing. Writing about Lacan's theory of desire, psychoanalyst Juliet Mitchell says:

> The object that is longed for only comes into existence as an object when it is lost to the baby or infant. Thus any satisfaction that might subsequently be attained will always contain this loss within it. Lacan refers to this dimension as "desire." . . . Desire persists as an effect of a primordial absence and it therefore indicates that, in this area, there is something fundamentally impossible about satisfaction itself.[1]

Desire—if we come to understand it—reveals the limitations of being human. We never can fulfill our desires in a literal or concrete way, because each attempt will include fresh desires. This is why desire leads to desire and is part of the reason why human beings are such a dissatisfied lot. Writer and Buddhist teacher Peter Matthiesen reminds us that the most ancient spiritual writings of India identified desire as a problem: "The Vedas already included the idea that mortal desire—since it implies lack—had no place in the highest state of being."[2] This quality of being insatiable links human desire to suffering in both Hindu and Buddhist teachings.

In Buddhism, especially, we find poignant, instructive metaphors for desire. One that has been useful clinically and personally is the image of the Hungry Ghost. In Buddhist mythology, there is a pictorial representation of what is called the Wheel of Life. Presented as a *mandala*, or circle, the wheel depicts the six realms or modes of existence that comprise the cycle of life and death. The realm of Hungry Ghosts is one of the hell realms—not the very lowest—and is populated by beings driven by rage and emptiness.

These realms on the Wheel of Life can be understood as psychological and/or actual states. That is, they can be seen as states of mind or as places. Here is the way a contemporary psychiatrist, in his account of a Buddhist approach to psychoanalysis, describes Hungry Ghosts: "Tormented by unfulfilled cravings and insatiably demanding impossible satisfactions, the Hungry Ghosts are searching for gratification for old unfulfilled needs whose time has passed."[3] Because these beings have identified themselves with insatiable longing, they are unable to recognize the difference between themselves and their desires. When we are driven by desire and fail to see into its nature, we become Hungry Ghosts—drifting through our lives without sustenance, because we constantly feel empty, always wanting something else. Unknowingly, we have been captured by desire itself.

The Object of Desire

If you are unconscious of your desires because you project them onto others and try to control those others to meet your needs, you easily can be captured by desire. Not knowing your wishes and wants, not knowing even that you have them, you become obsessed with being the object of someone else's desire. Then, instead of feeling yourself to be the subject of your own desire—a person doing and being—you feel as if you are controlled by what others need and want. Your own (often unconscious, hidden) desire is to be wanted, reassured, or praised by another.

How does this peculiar state come about? Earlier I talked about the primary split in our psyches between self and Other. Subjectivity is invested in both. Subpersonalities which are not-I (but which continue to be parts of the self) easily can be projected onto other people on a temporary or continuous basis. In infancy and childhood, they are necessarily and often continuously projected.

Picture the developing infant reflected in another's gaze or gesture. For a variety of reasons, and at any point along the developmental trajectory from infancy to adulthood, an individual may come to feel that reflections of the self are more exciting, vital, and necessary than the experience of an autonomous will or agency. Then the child gradually and unconsciously will narrow the ego complex to produce only the responses that seem to be desired by those important others—whether they are parents or peers—who are giving the sought-after reflections. Instead of developing a healthy autonomy, recognizing the self as an agent, the child functions to delight or please others. The ego complex becomes more and more constrained, until there may be no sense of free will at all. In place of the belief that one directs one's own desires and actions, there is a belief that one is controlled by others' beliefs, desires, and needs.

Many psychoanalysts—most prominently Alice Miller—have written about this kind of situation in the child of narcissistically wounded parents who require the child to be a reflection of themselves and their desires.[4] But I believe that this condition is not restricted to children of narcissistically wounded (and wounding) parents. The development of female gender identity and the female self contains much potential for this kind of outcome: to experience oneself as the object, rather than as the subject, of desire.

Of course, on some level, we all want to be desired. This aim is healthy when it leads to the capacity to give and take in an exchange of love—first with primary caregivers, later with chums and friends, and finally with partners or children of our own.[5] Fundamentally, I believe (differently from Lacan) that the impetus to become the *object* of desire—that is, to get positive reflections back from another—arises from a primary need to offer love and to feel that one's love is good. The psychoanalyst Harold Searles writes about this impetus in the following way:

> *Throughout most of the literature . . . concerning the psychogenesis of any variety of psychiatric illness — there is an almost exclusive emphasis upon the infant's (and child's) need to* receive *love, and upon the failure of those about him to* give *him the love he needed. What is usually overlooked is the fact that the infant and child has an equally great need, from the first, to express his own love to others. . . . My belief . . . is that the infant and child normally* gives, *and needs to* give, *at least as much as he receives.*[6]

For many different reasons, this normal need can be turned into a compulsion to be *seen* as lovable, exciting, worthy, or seductive.

In our society, such a shift occurs fairly commonly in the development of girls and women. As I said earlier, in place of feeling her own—especially competitive or sexual—desires, often a young woman will strive to be the object of desire. Repressing or ignoring the reality that this desire (to be desired) arises in herself, she feels trapped into complying with the demands and desires of others. Ways of appearing, acting, being are experienced as if they were controlled by others; in fact, they are under the control of the subjective Other and are projected onto another person or other people.

Disclaiming actions, wishes, and wants, such a person may sound and feel as if she had no ego complex. Actually, there *is* an ego complex, but it is consumed with wanting to be *reflected* in a certain way by others. If a person does not know her own desire, she is driven by desire unconsciously. This kind of experience often is described as unreal, without substance, feeling almost imaginary—like a Hungry Ghost. Instead of a direct sense of knowing and being, the self is experienced as *imitating* and *pretending*. Defending the ego complex is a *persona* (appearing to be what is wanted by the Other) that is inflexible and rigid, often compulsive, protecting consciousness from the rage and impotence that fuel the ego. This situation differs from psychoanalyst Donald Winnicott's concept of a defensive "false self" that protects an authentic "true self" that was unable to survive in an unempathic early environment. When female identity forms around being the object of desire, the earliest adaptive environment may have been good enough to promote the beginnings of a healthy ego complex, but the natural desire to be wanted has become so strong that it derails the development of autonomy. Confusedly, the ego forms around beliefs and images that are projected onto others and takes as a goal being an object of desire.[7]

In the following, through the story of Pandora, told from the female perspective, I describe how a girl or woman becomes the object of desire. Then, at the end of this section, I give a very brief account of a few themes that typically arise in connection with being a male object of desire. Mainly, I use a female narrative to illustrate the workings of our living myth of Pandora because it is a cultural reality.[8] As we shall see, women and men—all of us—promulgate the myth of female beauty, in which girls and women are induced to play the role of the object of desire.

Pandora as the First Woman

Earlier, I said that mythology is alive when it forms the basis of what we take to be reality. I gave the example of our contemporary myth of scientific realism to show how we rely on beliefs we do not understand and how we put our faith in mysterious scientific technology, about which we may know little or nothing. Similarly, the myth of female beauty—exemplified in the Greek story of Pandora—is alive in most modern societies of today's world. It does not matter whether you know anything of the actual story; the commodity of female beauty is used as a specific kind of power chip.

Pandora's story is about the patriarchal construction of Woman, literally and figuratively. As we shall see, this first woman is a prototype of contemporary Woman. Her story is about evil power; as we review it, we become conscious of some of the cultural and psychological roots of our need to make women into objects of desire.

Like Eve in the Garden of Eden, Pandora brings death into the world. She is the instigator of mortality for humans, and she also is the first mortal. Before her presence, all humans were male and immortal. What Pandora brought to those first Greek men was Trouble in the form of division—between male and female, between the immortal gods and the mortal humans. Here is a summary of Hesiod's account of the story, translated from the Greek by Richmond Lattimore.[9] Some of the story is paraphrased in my own words, and some is quoted from his translation.

Pandora is created as a punishment to Prometheus. Prometheus is a Titan (an old god) who created men from clay. Eventually he also gave men fire to help them develop civilization; this gift of fire was stolen from the gods, who were supposed to control its secrets. That Prometheus gave fire to men enraged Zeus, the god in charge of the Olympians, a newer race of gods who had defeated the Titans.

Although Zeus in some ways was pleased with the creation of humans (they offered gifts to the gods, for instance), he was outraged that Prometheus had shared with them one of the gods' secrets. Zeus now was compelled to reduce the power of men. To, Prometheus, the transgressor, Zeus says, "You are happy that you stole the fire and outwitted my thinking; but it will be a great sorrow to you and to men who come after. As the price of fire, I will give them an evil, and all men shall fondle this, their evil, close to their hearts, and take delight in it."

This evil would be Pandora, Woman. Zeus laughed loud and hard as he told the lowly god Hephaestus to mix earth and water and make a "desire-awakening maiden" with a face as beautiful as those of the immortal goddesses. This clay body Hephaestus was to infuse with strength and provide with a voice, but the goddesses were to give the creature beauty and skills. Athena was to teach her weaving. Aphrodite was to mist her head in a golden "endearment" and give her the cruelty of desire that wears out the body. Hermes was to impart a treacherous nature; in place of a heart, he was to set lies, flattery, and deceit. Hermes also gave this creature her name, *Pandora* ("many gifts"), because she had been given so many gifts by the Olympians, and because she was a gift to men. Pandora was to be for men a bane as powerful as fire had been a boon.

Before Woman was sent to earth, men had been living well. They had been without evil and disease, living in a paradise, free of laborious work. Although we do not have the complete record of this myth and so do not know the details of all the difficulties that Pandora brought to men, one extant fragment is illustrative.

Pandora's curiosity led her to dig up an old earthenware jar that long had been buried. She pried open its lid, and out poured the troubles of the world: death, disease, adversity. Hesiod recounts what Pandora released into the world: "The earth is full of evil things, and the sea is full of them. There are sicknesses that come to men by day, while in the night moving of themselves they haunt us, bringing sorrow to the mortals." As Pandora clamped down the lid of the jar, hope alone remained inside, so humans retain this one resource.[10]

Pandora now is remembered (erroneously) for opening a "box" that contained all evils. She has become a symbol of the disaster occasioned by rampant, impulsive curiosity. Few of us realize how much her story tells about the contemporary suffering of girls and women, about the unspoken and unspeakable way in which female beauty is made a commodity. This beauty—often the single socially condoned source of power that is openly offered to a female person entering maturity—may be assumed to be a woman's only legitimate resource. My earlier discussion of the female gender indicated that adolescent girls value being popular and looking good more than they value personal achievement, athletic prowess, or other forms of agentive development.[11] It is as if the curse of Zeus remains in effect to this day. Human beings are enthralled by a Pandora who is said to be beautiful but empty, seductive but untrustworthy, apparently fully human but in fact lacking a heart.

Although Pandora is a story about Woman, her story is not really about an actual woman or a woman's perspective. No woman could have created such a wholly unsympathetic figure, so perversely lacking in human values. Pandora is an anima figure—a man's dream lover who humiliates him with her beauty and manipulates him with her lies. If a man falls for such a creature, he must be wary of her power over him. If he does not fall for her, in the male power hierarchy he may not be viewed as legitimate. Remember that Zeus sent Pandora as a "desire-awakening maiden" to redress a power imbalance. Pandora is a pawn in the male power game; her story is not really about women. It is about competition among men.

The Double Bind of Female Beauty

When writer Naomi Wolf described our contemporary Beauty Myth in a recent helpful book about female appearance, she told a Pandora story. Although she was unaware of the myth's roots in Greek culture, she showed how we use scientific theories and language to support the Beauty Myth—the myth that female beauty is power. She illustrated her point with a sociobiological account of beauty. It went like this:

*The [B]eauty [M]yth tells a story: The quality called "beauty" objec-
tively and universally exists. Women must want to embody it and
men must want to possess women who embody it. This embodiment
is an imperative for women and not for men . . . because it is biological, sexual, and evolutionary: Strong men battle for beautiful
women, and beautiful women are more reproductively successful.* [12]

Although this account is perhaps less resonant emotionally
than the Greek story, it clearly demonstrates how the male hierarchy gives rise to the beauty game. That strong men battle for beautiful women is the curse of Zeus, from the perspective of Greek
mythology. The scientific myth says that beautiful women are
more "reproductively successful." What? replies Naomi Wolf.
Beauty is not universal; there is no standard for what is "beautiful."
Hence there can be no genetic or universal trait associated with
beauty. Moreover, anthropologists have shown that more
aggressive females are more reproductively successful. Certain
facts do not count when it comes to our contemporary Pandora
myth; it is the story itself that counts, retold now in "scientific"
language.

Let us return, then, to Hesiod's account of the Beauty Myth
and examine its premise: female beauty is an evil power. Most of us
(myself included) act as if we believe that female beauty is powerful. We engage in obsessive assessments of female bodies, reviewing the size and shape of lips, eyes, breasts, hips, legs, buttocks; the
texture of skin, hair, muscle; the specifics of slenderness. A woman
is an object (in her own and others' eyes) in such a ritual of body
analysis.

Pandora's story shows us how Zeus's curse is a double bind for
men and women—you are damned if you do and damned if you do
not. If a man believes that female beauty is power, he will have to
stay on guard with his trophy women; they are empty, deceitful,
manipulative. He could be humiliated. On the other hand, if he
does not evaluate women principally by their appearance, if he is

too awkward or disbelieving of the beautiful-but-empty account of women, then he risks being left out of the male hierarchy. An illustrative scene in Oliver Stone's recent movie, *Nixon*, shows an awkward, married Richard Nixon declining sex with a pretty young prostitute and so provoking anxiety in the men around him. What's wrong with this guy? The question is silently communicated among them.

For a woman, the stakes are even higher. If she identifies with the Pandora image, she must take on the label of beautiful but empty (i.e., "bimbo"). Even if she feels that the label does not fit, others will act as if it does, and she will have a hard time resisting their evaluation. The Pandora woman may *feel* powerful when she is a desire-awakening *maiden*, but as she begins to age, she will feel powerless and panicky. The clock and her appearance will compete, as she tries to stay youthful, slender, lovely. If she remains a Pandora into midlife, she will have ignored other strengths, failed to pursue achievements, creativity, or power of her own. When her youthful persona breaks down, she will uncover a Hungry Ghost. Although psychiatrist Mark Epstein is describing the Hungry Ghosts on the Wheel of Life in the following passage, he could be describing certain depressed midlife women: "They are beings who have uncovered a terrible emptiness within themselves, who cannot see the impossibility of correcting something that has already happened. Their ghostlike state represents their attachment to the past."[13]

If a young woman merely opposes the Pandora myth, without understanding it or breaking free of its double bind, she will be damned in a different way. Unwilling or unable to play the part of desire-awakening maiden, such a woman identifies with being an outsider to women (and perhaps to men as well). She "lets herself go." Unless she is very talented or very lucky, her oppositional stance is likely to lead to low self-esteem and fear of failure—failure to find a partner, especially. Whether she is heterosexual, homosexual, or bisexual, the oppositional Pandora is likely to be uncertain of her attractiveness and afraid of being left alone. For both men and women, identifying with the story leads to pain, while opposing the story (while still being in it) leads to different pain. Such is the nature of a double bind.

Gregory Bateson and others have studied double binds over the past couple of decades.[14] A double bind is a situation in which there is no right solution and at least two wrong ones. When people feel trapped in a double bind, they feel like they are going crazy, because it appears that there should be a "right" way to proceed, but there is none. Whether you are male or female, Pandora is dangerous and untrustworthy. But if you reject the drama of female beauty (without examining its premises), then you will tend to feel left out of the power game of patriarchy, no matter what your sex.

There is only one way to defeat this or any other double bind. It is necessary to stop feeling trapped within it, stop seeing it as reality. In order to do this, usually people must become conscious of the origins and meanings of the bind. The double bind is an unconscious manipulation that hooks people into trying to find a solution to an insoluble problem. For example, the parent who fears a growing child's departure from home unconsciously may set up a double bind. If the child leaves home, the parent will be unhappy because the parent will be lonely. If the child does not leave home, the parent will be unhappy because it will be a sign that the family has failed to produce an autonomous adult. Under such circumstances, some children have emotional breakdowns because they feel awful about both alternatives: staying at home or leaving home. Among human beings, double binds often arise out of jealousies, competition, and unmet needs.

The double bind of female beauty, the Pandora myth, is a punishment to both sexes. It keeps us locked in a reality that harms our relationships and our selves, as we cast gender stories into plots and subplots that require men and women to be enemies and/or to be mutually defeated.

Stepping Outside the Pandora Myth

To acknowledge the living power of the Pandora myth is to recognize the ways in which it captures us. Then we can begin to step outside the double bind of female beauty and resist this narrative of the object of desire. Pandora is a story about beauty and power. Let us examine these two components from a postmodern Jungian perspective, using what we have learned about gender and contrasexuality.

What is beauty? From a constructivist perspective, beauty lies mostly in the eye of the beholder. No single standard of beauty reigns among people everywhere; there is no archetype of personal beauty. There is no rationale for linking beauty to slenderness, except as fashion may demand it.

You yourself may have noted how beauty inevitably is colored by your own emotions. At one moment—when you are feeling joyful, well-fed, content, excited—your lover seems to you radiant and vital; then, only a few moments later, the same person appears dull, sloppy, tired, or boring. The subjective factor of our contrasexuality colors our perceptions in a general way, motivating us toward or away from this or that behavior or gesture in another; but even our passing moods affect our perceptions. When we recognize how much of our attraction and desire arises from our own feelings and fantasies, we begin to stop seeing ourselves as literal objects of desire.

The knowledge of our own contribution to our perceptions should startle us and awaken us to how much we are the agents of our desires, rather than desires arising as a result of external stimuli *per se*. Jung says of this subjective factor:

> *Every new representation, be it a perception or a spontaneous thought, arouses associations which derive from the storehouse of memory. These leap immediately into consciousness, producing the complex picture of an "impression," though this is already a sort of in-*

terpretation. *The unconscious disposition upon which the quality of the impression depends is what I call the "subjective factor."*

He continues,

The prominence of the subjective factor does not imply a personal subjectivism . . . *The psyche and its structure are real enough. They even transform material objects into psychic images . . . They do not perceive waves, but sound; not wave-lengths, but colours. Existence is as we see and understand it. There are innumerable things that can be seen, felt and understood in a great variety of ways.*[15]

When we become deeply aware of this subjective factor, we can begin to take different perspectives in viewing things, moving away from the belief that we only "call 'em as we see 'em" or "call 'em as they are." As we recognize how the object of desire arises within us, we begin to free ourselves from the Pandora myth that has cursed humankind.

But I do not want to leap ahead too quickly. Although our society has undergone many changes in gender roles and meaning over the past two decades, we have not changed the Beauty Myth. The pains and miseries of Pandora perhaps are more prevalent now than ever, as Mary Pipher illustrates so clearly in *Reviving Ophelia*, an account of the lives of adolescent daughters in America.[16] Adolescent girls quickly learn to measure their personal worth in terms of their appearance. At the same time, we all support a cosmetic and fashion industry with a gross annual income of some trillion dollars. Through it, women manipulate their bodies, faces, and hair, sometimes even dangerously (as a recent scandal concerning breast implants tragically illustrates). Being thin has become an obsession, an illness, among girls as young as early elementary school, who style themselves after anorexic fashion models. Eating disorders and disordered eating have reached almost epidemic proportions among white, middle-class, American girls and young women. As other races, classes, and societies imitate white American fashion, they too fall prey to these disorders. Weight Watchers of America enrolls women in twelve thousand classes weekly across our country, although research has demonstrated the general failure of dieting.[17]

My recent book about couples, *You're Not What I Expected*, deals at length with contemporary problems in female sexual desire, noting that

> We have vast archives of men's depictions of their dream lovers, and male views of women's lives are often the only resource some people have for portraits of women's desire. Circe, Pandora, Aphrodite, and Eve are illustrations of "classical" dream-lover depictions of female desire, and sex, lies and videotape and Presumed Innocent are contemporary examples from movies. These and countless others depict female sexuality from a male perspective, giving nuance and meaning through the lenses of men's fantasies about female desire.[18]

Because of the absence of women's accounts of female sexual desire, women and men alike are lost and confused about its nature. In male-dominated societies, what feels good for girls and women erotically and sexually has been largely concealed.

At the core of these issues is a confusion between being the object and being the subject of desire. Because female sexual desire is objectified as "how I need to look" rather than experienced as "how I want to feel," girls and women rarely are informed about their own bodies and their sexual responses. If they know about these responses, that knowledge nevertheless is deemed less important than looking a certain way. As young as elementary-school age, girls may become concerned with weight, appearance, dress. By the time that reproductive hormones influence sexual arousal, many young women are convinced that appearance is the most important predictor of a happy life. At any age, a woman may try to *look* sexy in order to feel sexual, while, in the sexual arena, remaining confused by the question "What do *you* want?"

Because our society has been captured by the Pandora myth, we indoctrinate young men and women in the ritual of objectifying the female body. The female body is on display *everywhere*. Billboards, television commercials, magazines, movies, and newspapers exhibit thousands of Pandora images, used to sell all sorts of commodities. What they sell best, though, is the object of desire—female beauty. Because of our ability to reproduce images in media now, we may be worse off than earlier societies in terms of the Pandora myth. So ubiquitous is the desire-awakening maiden that we barely notice her pervasive effects on our lives.

Naomi Wolf emphasizes the objectification of the female body in the development of female sexuality: "Girls learn to watch their sex along with the boys; that takes up the space that should be devoted to finding out about what they are wanting, and reading and writing about it, seeking it and getting it. Sex is held hostage by beauty and its ransom terms are engraved in girls' minds early and deeply."[19] Adolescents form their gendered selves around beliefs concerning, and images of, the female body as an object of desire. Feeling empty rather than authoritative concerning her own sexuality, a female person becomes confused. Instead of knowing what *she* wants, she tends to absorb the views projected onto her by others. Although a girl may not have the slightest idea of her own sexual pleasure or even of the actual effects she has in an erotic situation, she may internalize others' views of her as bad, seductive, "castrating," or manipulative. Without a clear erotic self-image, a girl may believe what is implied and said about her, simply because she does not know any other reality.

Among the many losses in the Pandora story is the loss of the female person as a sexual partner. Many men experience their female partners as adrift or unresponsive and blame themselves for this situation. (In lesbian couples, the problem of female sexual desire generally is better understood, although it may not be better solved.) Because a man learned in his youth what gives him sexual pleasure and how to reach that pleasure, he can feel sexual desire.

He assumes that every healthy person feels it. If he sees little or no evidence of this in his partner, he will tend to conclude that she is not attracted to him, that he has done or said something wrong. If he asks about this, his partner usually will respond in the affirmative—that he has (and there is always something to be found wrong in one's partner)—because she also does not know how else to explain her lack of desire.

When couples go off into their own dark analyses of the absence of female sexual desire, they often end up telling the Pandora story. The woman is seen as empty, deceptive, manipulative, or lying. Her attractiveness is understood as a power chip, brokering things like money and decision making. In this kind of dark exchange, projective identification often is implicated, as the unconscious aspects of the woman's contrasexuality (in the form of male power figures, positive or negative) fuse with the unconscious contrasexuality of the man (in the form of manipulative desire-awakening maidens). In various ways, both project and internalize aspects of the Pandora story until they feel enraged and hurt. This problem is widespread and well known in heterosexual sexual relations.

If we look back to the Pandora story, we find that men—once they have accepted Pandora—are defeated by the gods. They believe that female beauty equals power, lies, manipulation. They must bring this beauty under their control. This preoccupies them, leading them to compete with other men for possession of a beautiful woman, and to feel helpless and humiliated in her presence.

According to researcher and writer Tim Beneke, justification and rationalization of rape are common among men in all walks of life in our society.[20] We know from studies of college students that such justifications are common among both male and female students. Beneke, who has investigated men's attitudes toward rape, was shocked to discover, after working to rehabilitate male rapists, that his own attitudes concerning female beauty were reflected in the ways that rapists think. The underlying assumption shared by him and the rapists was that rape cannot be prevented and some-times is necessary, because men cannot control their sexual urges in the presence of a "seductive"—that is, powerful—female per-son (even if she is a child).

This view of female appearance as the instigating factor in rape was voiced repeatedly as Beneke interviewed hundreds of men— lawyers who tried rapists, judges who ruled in their cases, and or-dinary guys who would have nothing to do with literal rape. The same story was related by rapists themselves. Beneke began to see how we share a myth that, because of the powerful effect of female appearance, rape is natural and even necessary. He examined tele-vision, movies, advertising, and newspapers and found, especially in jokes and cartoons, countless depictions of the power of female appearance over men and of men as victims of this power.

I was fascinated by Beneke's study, because I realized that he had uncovered the Pandora story without any knowledge of Greek myths. He had uncovered the myth in the archetypal themes of his interviews. The men he interviewed were driven by a psychologi-cal complex, a contrasexual complex, that contained various images and beliefs depicting the female person as negatively powerful—empty, deceitful, enraged—and as exerting this power through her appearance.

Here is an excerpt from an interview with a man called "Jay." He is presented as an ordinary guy from Pittsburgh, who says he never would rape a woman, because "it's wrong and unlawful," not because he does not desire it. When asked about what he feels when he sees a sexy woman, Jay replies:

> *Let's say I see a woman and she looks really pretty and really clean and sexy, and she's giving off very feminine, sexy vibes, I think "Wow, I would love to make love to her," but I know she's not really interested. It's a tease. A lot of times a woman knows that she's look-ing really good and she'll use that and flaunt it, and it makes me feel like she's laughing at me and I feel degraded . . . I don't like the feel-*

ing that I'm supposed to stand there and take it . . . It's a feeling of hu-
miliation, because the woman has forced me to turn off my feelings
and react in a way that I really don't want to.[21]

Jay is living the myth of Pandora in a modern context. Although he is aware of how he is "supposed" to think about women
and that the wish to rape "should not" be a part of what he feels,
he experiences the woman's beauty as humiliating. He sees the
"trick" in the way she looks. He knows that "she knows she's looking really good" and that she wants to "use that and flaunt it."
What Jay does not know is that he is playing out a double bind, one
that has pervaded Western male-dominated societies since the
time of the ancient Greeks. If he embraces this Pandora myth, he
will not be able to trust a woman. If he does not embrace it, he will
not be trusted by men.

While women do not know that the beauty-power game is
more about men than about themselves, and while they do not
know all its codes and hidden messages, most men are insiders.
They have been working on this Pandora theme, in their fantasies
and with their male peers, for almost as long as they have known
sexual desire. Whether or not men are sexually attracted to
women, they know this story. They have heard how a beautiful
woman uses her power to humiliate a man. They have heard that
women are manipulative, that "no" can mean "yes," and that
women do not play by "the rules" when it comes to sex.[22] Many
men are deeply and fundamentally convinced that the desire-
awakening maiden should not be trusted. She is about power:
power over men and power over other women who compete
with her.

This myth of female beauty leaves men little freedom. As I
have worked with men in psychotherapy, I have seen how much
they relax and how relieved they feel when they step outside the
Pandora story. They discover a great deal about themselves, increase their trust of other men, and begin a dialogue about sexual

partnership, one in which they recognize—often for the first time—how much about female sexuality has been obscured.

Instead of remaining stuck in being the object of desire, it is possible to become the subject of one's own desire. Before looking at the specifics of how that can occur, however, let us return to the problem of how we see and understand gender and sexual desire. First, let me review some problems associated with being a male object of desire. Because of our cultural narratives about gender, nuances and meanings are different for males and females, but they also are somewhat similar. When a man has identified with being the object of desire—often the object of his mother's fantasies of power and intelligence—he loses the sense of himself as an active agent in his own life. He becomes unable to feel what he wants, feeling instead that he always is trying to please another. He has fallen into the projection of a woman's contrasexuality, because she (knowingly or unknowingly) demanded that he be wonderful, powerful, perfect, seductive, in order to meet her desires. Such a male person will come to feel trapped in a hall of mirrors, needing to be seen and regarded in particular ways in order to feel alive.

The main reason why I analyzed the female object of desire, as I said earlier, is that it is a major aspect of our culture. You can see every day how this myth grips us and seems to be reality. I hope you also can see the value of a postmodern approach to Pandora. If we were realists, we would be stuck in the sociobiological story that men want to possess beautiful women because they are more re-productively successful. We would feel helpless about heterosexual equality, believing that men and women never would be able to trust each another. We might find ourselves assuming that those few desire-awakening maidens available in any one place must be looked upon as trophies. We might claim that, around men, women should be protective of their real feelings, because men only want sex, not relationship. And so on.

As Jungians informed by hermeneutics and constructivism, we can tell a different story. First, we can see that a myth is a grand story about reality. Myths explain how we got here, why we are here, where we are going, why it is difficult, and how we can ease the path. Myths change as our understanding of life evolves and changes. No myth—not even our current scientific myth—is a perfectly accurate account of reality.

Third, as Jungians we know that people are never more than minimally conscious. We know that we are unconscious of the myths we live by until they give us so much pain as to awaken us to the possibility that they are *accounts* of reality, not reality itself. Whether or not we become conscious, we get the pain. Myths become painful when we have outgrown them but continue trying to force our experiences into them. Many of the personal myths we assimilated in our childhoods are inadequate to the complexity of adult life, but we try to fit our experiences into them anyway.

As a result of the recent wave of feminism, we have outgrown the Pandora myth. We now can step outside it and see it as a metaphor for the double bind of female beauty. Recognizing myth as metaphor frees us to use it for our own development, to see where we fall into it and why. Although it is very difficult to examine a living myth, because we function day by day believing it to be reality, we can examine a dying myth. Dying myths (most myths never die wholly) are transformed into metaphors, and we can see them as psychological images, as reflections of ourselves. Above, as we used the Pandora story to understand something about our erotic desires, we could see the assumptions and attitudes that we unknowingly impose on our experiences of the opposite sex; we could see the problem of sexual desire in a new light. Revealing the myths we live by, becoming conscious that they are accounts that have been taken to be reality, is the core of effective psychotherapy. As we shall see in the next section, transforming myth into metaphor releases us to be the subject of our own desires. In essence, we are engaged in a process of uncursing Pandora by releasing female beauty from a double bind.

CHAPTER FOUR

The Subject of Desire

Psychotherapy is a retelling of a life. When client and therapist reach what they call the "end" of therapy—although it is not by any means the end of the treatment, which, if successful, should go on forever—they have reformulated and recast the client's life into new meanings. Much that previously was myth has become metaphor. Much that had been projected onto others now is considered a part of the client's own subjective life. What had been taken as reality now is seen as an account of reality, one based in emotional meanings.

Gradually client and therapist have become conscious of the subjective origins of images, beliefs, and attitudes which had been viewed as true and natural but which now are seen as the emotional intelligence of an earlier adaptation to life. Although the client's myth was the story of one life, it also was the story of life in general.

Most of the myths I hear in therapy are composed of the unwritten and unspoken fantasies, fears, and ideals of a particular family of origin. No matter how perverse or bizarre these family myths may seem, they are human and understandable because the conflicts and constraints of human life operate within us all. Jung identified one of these universals when he noted how we all tend to live out the unlived lives of our parents—the "Once upon a time, there was a King and a Queen" of our particular story.[1] Those powerful desires or foibles, excluded from our parents' personalities and projected into our own, direct us into dramas which remain unconscious until we become aware of the scripts. The great majority of people, in our society and elsewhere, simply live out these embedded stories as if they were reality.

When people come to psychotherapy, they do not come to change their myths. They come because they are suffering, often because something in their psychological complexes is causing pain to themselves or others. Often some kind of troublesome myth (not regarded as such) is part of the problem.

For example, if you grew up with a father who never made enough money to pay the bills, who perpetually focused on finances, and who seemed always to be burdened with money worries, you likely developed a (positive or negative) preoccupation with money. Suppose you come to psychotherapy for reasons apparently unconnected with money—that you are having problems disciplining your adolescent children, for instance. But I notice that you talk a lot about money. I ask, "Why is money so important to you?" You likely would answer, "Doesn't everybody talk about money? Isn't it just natural to be preoccupied with money these days?" I hear that reply—"Isn't it natural?"—in response to queries concerning all kinds of unique and obscure preoccupations. No matter how peculiar the symptom, if the myth surrounding it is treated as reality, the person will be convinced that her or his desire is only natural.

Recall that desire contains within it the seed of dissatisfaction, the experience of something missing. All family and cultural myths compel us toward or away from certain desires. When our psychological complexes are weighted with unfulfilled parental desire, they are likely to be relentlessly compelling. From the surface, the underlying meaning may be difficult to assess. Desires can be expressed in fears and phobias, in ideals and ambitions, in needs for admiration and reassurance. When parents regularly have implied that their children must admire the parents and never see them as wrong or mistaken, a child over a lifetime may admire something as bizarre as the parent's criminality. When parental desire is projected chronically and unconsciously onto a particular child, that child will carry a strong positive or negative longing, surrounded by a myth or story that rationalizes the child's obsession.

Some commonplace mythic obsessions come from collective stories, as we just saw in the Pandora myth. Obsessive and compulsive strivings for female beauty are explained as entirely natural, no matter how bizarre they may be. "Why do you want to be so thin?" I have asked young women starving themselves, making themselves vomit, overusing laxatives, and overexercising. "Doesn't everyone want to be thin?" they reply. Indeed, if one lives, as most of us do, within the Pandora myth, everyone does want to be thin. After all, even the Duchess of Windsor once said that it was impossible to be too rich or too thin. Similar justifications for cosmetic surgery, breast implants, and compulsive shopping can be generated from the story that female beauty is power. In order to transform the Pandora myth into metaphor, in order to step outside it and see what the story means, we have to feel its double bind and begin to see it as a false account, not reality.

Changing Myth through Psychotherapy

One of my tasks in therapy is to help people appreciate the human origins of all accounts of reality. When people are creating pain and suffering by attempting to sustain their psychological complexes when different adaptation is demanded, they do not engage in philosophical debates. Myth becomes a practical matter. Obviously, we all need myth. It provides the context for what we take to be fact and truth. All societies use mythology to promote certain ways of living, especially in regard to gender roles and specializations.

A person in therapy cannot surrender an old myth until he or she can trust a new account of reality. This new account has to encompass and reorganize the emotional reality of the painful myth. The client and I will go through several stages or steps in confronting the old myth, exposing the desires hidden there, and revealing the metaphors and their meanings. Gradually we begin to tell a new story, a new myth, about how to understand and see that client's life.

In the outset of psychotherapy or analysis, the interactive field (transference and countertransference) is colored by different and conflicting desires on the part of both therapist and client. On one level, there is a desire to recognize and accept each other as human beings, as companions in the human realm. On another level, both of us have a desire to repeat the specifics of earlier important emotional adaptation, to enact our complexes—no matter how painful—because they are perceived as reality. For myself, as therapist, this wish is mediated by my analysis, training, and clinical experience. Yet my personality is structured by unconscious complexes; and, since human emotions are universal, my complexes can be triggered by someone else's enactments. My training and knowledge must assist me in seeing and understanding what is happening. On still another level, both of us want me to indicate a way out of the pain and suffering, toward new development.

Without going into the details of how these levels of transference work, I want to point out that, at the start of a psychotherapy, certain things work in favor of the client's change and development, and certain things work against them. On the positive side is our common humanity, the ways in which we can understand and relate because we both are more human than otherwise. Also on the positive side is the client's motivation for development—the inherent striving for greater coherence, differentiation, integration, purpose, and meaning that Jung calls "individuation." On the negative side is the tendency of the client to experience much of what I say and do as if I, too, were caught and limited by the painful myth that he or she brings to psychotherapy. No matter how far outside that reality I currently live, in order to assist the client in confronting and seeing through it I have to enter its emotional terrain and understand it through my own emotional intelligence. I cannot go into the details of how this happens here. My capacity to help, however, is based upon my ability to chart the subjective terrain of complexes within the prevailing myth of a painful reality. This involves working against "nature" (as Jung says of consciousness), in that what has seemed most natural has to be turned upside down and inside out and perceived as a fundamental problem.

My task is to open a transcendent function or a dialogical space, as I shall explain in a moment, between the experience of an impulse or conflict and the way it has been symbolized within the prevailing myth.[2] This will allow the client to see this experience in a new way. Complexes and mythic realities circumvent our capacity to be conscious. We are made in such a way that we reproduce emotional adaptation without reviewing it too closely. To open the space of self-awareness between the experience and the symbol is a task that is carried out after an old myth begins to break down.

In order to change something as fundamental as the basis of reality, people have to trust that they are being accepted, seen, and protected in exactly the ways in which their early relationships failed. Because of the levels and types of transference in psychotherapy, to create this fundamental trust in the therapeutic environment requires time, skill, and a secure ethical foundation. Current social and political reactions against long-term psychotherapy[3] are expressions of scientific realism, without an understanding of postmodernism. For instance, to believe that people can change their psychological functioning simply by taking a medication[4] or learning how to reorganize cognitive patterns[5] is to ignore the limitations of human knowledge. The scientific realism of modernity presumes that human knowledge rests upon impersonal functions that can be changed and adjusted without achieving self-recognition. Serotonin levels and negative self-talk certainly affect our capacity to pay attention and be alert, but they do not create the myth within which we live, nor can they change it.

As we see clearly through the lens of postmodernism, in order to change our minds and realities, we need to know how we live subjectively. The constraints of human embodiment, our species' attachment and dependency needs, our limited lifespan, and our self-recognized death, together make it very difficult for us to change our primary emotional intelligence. This changes only as the self changes, and the self changes (by reorganizing primary attitudes and beliefs) only through relationship.

Knowing that human beings never can get beyond mythology—our best account of reality at a given moment—we are better able to examine the implications of particular myths. When collective myths begin to fail, they no longer provide what people need in order to develop emotionally and psychologically. A dying myth inhibits and oppresses rather than inspires, prompting us to feel cut off and confused about our own emotional responses. In everyday life and in psychotherapy, I have felt the harm of dominance myths—stories that justify the power of certain people over others. These stories may have had survival value for human beings for millennia, as we struggled to gain control over dangerous aspects of our environment. But such stories quickly are becoming obsolete, as our species overpopulates the planet and must become more cooperative and accepting of limits.

When we, personally or collectively, continue to live an outgrown myth, it appears as psychopathology—painful symptoms. Pandora is an example of a troublesome dominance myth. It creates a double bind in regard to female beauty and produces maladaptive fantasies concerning dominance and submission between men and women. Surely we have seen enough starving girls and women to know how painful Pandora's symptoms are. Becoming aware of our symptomatic expressions, of how we create and sustain them, we begin to see myth as metaphor. No longer is

Pandora a story about the power of female beauty. Now it is a metaphor for the double bind of female beauty. Movement from living within a harmful myth to recognizing its symbolic meaning as metaphor is the process underlying successful analysis or psychotherapy.

Transcendent Function

As psychiatrist and Jungian analyst Anthony Stevens stated in *The Two-Million-Year-Old Self*, "To Jung, mental illness resulted from a loss of contact between the subjective and objective psyches, between conscious and unconscious personalities, between the ego and the Self. The way of healing was to bring the two sides together—in other words[,] to activate the psychic function which he called transcendent."[6] To restate this in postmodern terms, we are psychologically healthy when we recognize the link between our subjective life and that which we perceive as objective—between the mood or dream ("in here") and the world ("out there"). Ultimately there is no strong line between an in-here and out-there because all that we know is grounded in our own perceptions, interpretations, knowledge.

Our subjective impressions link us to what we regard as objective. Already, as Jung says, they are "a sort of interpretation." When we keep this fact strongly in our awareness, we are rooted in the human realm, recognizing our limitations. When we lose track of it and believe that reality is out there or in here and we can see or know it directly, we fall into fears and dangers.

Here is an example of an individual in psychotherapy who is caught in a realist bind. The patient

> knew the therapist, who had begun the hour three minutes late, did so because he preferred the patient whose hour preceded this patient's. . . . Attempts on the part of the therapist to understand why the patient interpreted the lateness in this particular way were met with exasperation. The patient accused the therapist of relying on textbook interpretations to deny the obvious.[7]

For this patient, feelings are facts. They are not emotional responses to be understood. There is no space between the experience of the therapist's lateness and the symbol—the complex-laden image of the rejecting therapist. The patient is a realist who believes that gut feelings deliver the facts. Of this kind of realism, psychoanalyst Thomas Ogden, who wrote the above passage, says, "With the collapse of the distinction between symbol and symbolized, there is no room in which to 'entertain' ideas and feelings." Under these circumstances, a relationship "takes on a deadly serious quality; illusion becomes delusion; thoughts become plans; feelings become impending actions . . . play becomes compulsion."[8] This is how—when one becomes a naïve realist, lacking any awareness of her or his own subjectivity—mental illness arises. Always, in the space between an experience and its representation (as an image or expression), there stands a human being who wants, wills, or knows something. In every impression, perception, action, or feeling, there is a subject who is doing something.

The self-awareness gained in psychotherapy, once symptoms have abated, provides us with an internal "space" in which to recognize ourselves as subjects. This space offers a perspective within which we can examine beliefs from several angles, becoming more inquisitive and modest about what we see as "true." Through this transcendent function, we come to recognize that our sense of what is real depends upon seeing things in a particular way, and that our vision of things always is colored by our own associations and emotions.

No longer are things "just natural" or simply as "they are." With regard to female appearance, for example, the double bind disappears and a choice exists—to step into a particular frame of reference or to stay out of it. If you are a woman, you may find that looking good feels "as if" you are powerful, without believing that it makes you powerful. If you are a man, you may feel "as if" you are more masculine being with an attractive woman, but such a feeling is not an essential aspect of your masculinity. And if you choose not to play the Pandora game, you recognize the implications of your choice without feeling that the choice is a deadly serious matter.

In analyzing the Pandora story, we see that, in a male-dominated society, a beautiful woman stands for something—is a metaphor. She is a metaphor for certain kinds of power in a particular power game. You can play with the metaphor if you are conscious of it, although you may never be entirely free of the story if it has long been a part of your reality.

A thirty-year-old man whom I saw in therapy came to realize that a beautiful woman would not enhance his power or substitute for accomplishments. It took him almost three years of intensive analytic work to see that many of his power fantasies were projected onto attractive women and that these fantasies had nothing to do with the women themselves. He gradually came to see that dating beautiful women was helping him feel "as if" he were more manly without making him more of a man. With this self-knowledge, he chose a woman to be his special companion, hoping that eventually they would marry.

From among the intelligent, attractive women he was dating, the client chose the one who, to him, was the most beautiful. He recognized what he was doing. The symbolic value of her appearance remained more important to him than other needs which would have been filled better by another woman. He also acknowledged (because it came up in his dreams) that he feared his partner's aging—the wrinkling of her skin and the thinning of her hair. He hoped that eventually other aspects of their life together would remedy this deficit in his masculinity, which seemed to demand female beauty. Although this man had not become entirely free of the myth of female beauty, he had been able to step back from believing literally that a beautiful woman would satisfy his desire for greater power and manliness.

When we recognize that our most cherished beliefs and desires rest upon seeing things as if they were true, we begin to know ourselves as the subject of our own desires. We begin to look into the mirror of self-recognition and see who has been giving us so much trouble. To think that these problems might be "nothing until we call them" is both shocking and liberating. It is shocking to think that our own subjectivity can evoke a world of response. On the other hand, it is freeing to think that we can change a lot of what takes place in our lives by changing our own attitudes and responses.

The new mythology that is established in a successful psychotherapy is like the lesson of Buddhist hell. The lowest realm of hell on the Wheel of Life is composed of beings who are driven by fear, aggression, rage, and pain. They are restless and unable to do anything to soothe themselves. The bodhisattva, or saintly figure, who accompanies those in hell is a figure holding a mirror. Like an effective therapist, this bodhisattva is there to help those in hell see themselves. When they recognize themselves as creating the conditions from which they suffer, they will be liberated. This kind of self-awareness—seeing the large part we play in making things what they are—is quite different from being self-conscious or overly analytical.

Thomas Ogden calls this awareness the "dialogical space," and Jung calls it the "transcendent function."[9] They describe it as the capacity to hold opposites in tension, without believing that there is one "right" way. Not-knowing takes precedence over knowing, and holding a question open takes precedence over quick closure on meaning. In the world of self-awareness, we come to value uncertainty.

Being aware of my own desires, rather than focusing on what I must or should do, results in a more centered, open approach to experience. If I choose not to engage in a particular power game, for example, I nevertheless do not belittle those who do so, because I can see their motives in myself. If I am playful about this, I can handle conflicts with a light touch, because I am not blaming myself or another.

In refusing to be a naïve realist, I shall encounter opportunities for development, for seeing myself and others more empathically. This is the attitude that is engendered in a postmodern analytical psychology, in its theory and its practice.

Myth and Postmodernism

If we fail to address human universals in emotional life—the ways in which we all are constrained by our emotions, our relational dependence, and our embodiment—we shall end up with a psychology of isolated individuals, each convinced that he or she is profoundly unknowable to the others. On the other hand, if we approach the study of universals without regard for subjective and sociocultural aspects of meaning, we shall bog down in a psychologically dangerous type of realism.

In order to experience ourselves as the subjects of our own desires, we need a framework that allows us to probe the limits of our myths. Jung's psychology of complexes is extraordinarily helpful in revealing how we are driven by our desires and what these desires mean. Hermeneutics and constructivism also are helpful, in that they demand that we notice the dialogical space between the symbol and the symbolized, whether we are dealing with biology or psychoanalysis. They also awaken us to the interplay of power and privilege that accompanies our cultural myths.

When we are able to break down harmful myths and use their images as metaphors for aspects of ourselves, then we see ourselves within the domain of human responsibility, examining what it means to be an engaged, responsible *person*. Obviously this is different from being a god or goddess, a Hungry Ghost, an animal, or a victim.

In the human realm, there is enormous potential for change, because we can discover directly how we are the subjects of our own desires. This is a fundamental principle of all forms of psychoanalysis, but it is also an ancient teaching of the Buddha: "One is the creator of oneself . . . one 'is of one's own making . . . whatever one does, good or bad, one will become heir to that.'"[10] Through self-awareness and self-knowledge, we humans can discover how we create ourselves and how we can alleviate our suffering. This capacity permits us to change our fate.

In a postmodern analysis of myth, we discover and rediscover the boundaries between the unchangeable and the changeable in our lives, between constraints and freedoms. This is the heart of my practice of analytical psychology: I continue to learn how to retell the stories of all the beings in the human realm.

Notes

Foreword

1. Virginia Woolf, *A Room of One's Own* (Middlesex, England: Penguin Books, 1928), 103.
2. Polly Young-Eisendrath and Florence Wiedemann, *Female Authority: Empowering Women through Psychotherapy* (New York: Guilford Press, 1987).
3. C. G. Jung, *Letters* vol. I (Princeton, N.J.: Princeton University Press, 1973), 495.
4. C. G. Jung, *Memories, Dreams, Reflections*, ed. A. Jaffe (New York: Pantheon, 1963), 293–98, 314–15, 327–59; David H. Rosen, *The Tao of Jung: The Way of Integrity* (New York: Viking, 1996), 96–97, 116–60.
5. Verena Kast, *The Nature of Loving: Patterns of Human Relationship*, trans. B. Matthews (Wilmette, Ill.: Chiron Publications, 1986); June Singer *Androgyny: Toward a New Theory of Sexuality* (New York: Anchor Books, 1977); Demaris Wehr, *Jung and Feminism: Liberating Archetypes* (Boston: Beacon Press, 1987).
6. Mary Pipher, *Reviving Ophelia: Saving the Selves of Adolescent Girls* (New York: Putnam, 1994).
7. Wehr, *Jung and Feminism*, 125.

Chapter 1.
The Problem of Realism in Analytical Psychology

1. For an overview of the implications of different metatheories for the way we do science and history, in regard to the nature of "truth," W. F. Overton, "World Views and Their Influence on Psychological Theory and

Research: Kuhn-Lakatos-Laudan," in *Advances in Child Development and Behavior*, ed. H. W. Reese, 18:191–226 (New York: Academic Press, 1984); W. F. Overton, "Historical and Contemporary Perspectives on Developmental Theory and Research Strategies," in *Visions of Aesthetics, the Environment, and Development: The Legacy of Joachim Wohlwill*, ed. R. Downs, L. Liben, and D. Palermo, 263–311 (Hillsdale, N.J.: Lawrence Erlbaum, 1991); W. F. Overton, "The Structure of Developmental Theory," in *Advances in Child Development and Behavior*, ed. H. W. Reese, 23:1–37 (New York: Academic Press, 1991); W. F. Overton, "The Arrow of Time and the Cycle of Time: Concepts of Change, Cognition, and Embodiment," *Psychological Inquiry* 5, no. 3 (1994): 215–37.

2. Sociobiologists suggest that polygamy has evolutionary advantages in certain circumstances, due to the increased probability of passing one's genes onto the next generation. K. B. MacDonald, *Social and Personality Development: An Evolutionary Synthesis* (New York: Plenum Press, 1988), ch. 5. R. Trivers, "Parent-Offspring Conflict," *American Zoologist* 14 (1974): 249–64, for a cost-benefit analysis of reproduction. J. Belsky, L. Steinberg, and P. Drapper, "Childhood Experience, Interpersonal Development, and Reproductive Strategies: An Evolutionary Theory of Socialization," *Child Development* 62 (1991): 647–70. Two recent examples of the genetic perspective on criminology include: P. A. Brennan and S. A. Mednick, "Genetic Perspectives on Crime," *Acta Psychiatrica Scandinavia* 370 (1993): 19–26; and P. O. Alm, M. Alm, K. Humble, J. Leppert, S. Sorensen, L. Lidberg, and L. Oreland, "Criminality and Platelet Monoamine Oxidase Activity in Former Juvenile Delinquents as Adults," *Acta Psychiatrica Scandinavia* 89 (1994): 41–45.

3. It has been argued effectively that metaphor is not simply a heuristic device and that it is not reducible to material explanation. Instead, metaphor is central to the scientific research process. Metaphor introduces greater coherence, organization, and plausibility into scientific observations. W. F. Overton, "Metaphor, Recursive Systems, and Paradox in Science and Developmental Theory," in *Advances in Child Development and Behavior*, ed. H. W. Reese, 23:59–71 (New York: Academic Press, 1991).

4. Realists reject the interpretive stance because they fear that, if interpretation is the basis of knowledge, any individual could make any claim, and all claims would be equally valid; this would lead to relativism and solipsism. The goal of science, however, is to establish a systematic body of knowledge which is controlled by methods of observation and inter-

pretation. Interpretation brings greater order, coherence, generality, and plausibility to empirical observations. Furthermore, interpretations can be judged in terms of their scope and lack of contradictions; thus, from the perspective of any discipline, not all interpretations are equally valid. Overton, "Historical and Contemporary Perspectives"; Overton, "Metaphor, Recursive Systems, and Paradox"; and Overton, "Structure of Developmental Theory."

5. Among theories which depict development as proceeding through universal stages are: Erik Erikson, *Identity and the Life Cycle* (New York: W. W. Norton, 1980); the archetypal theory of C. G. Jung, *The Collected Works of C. G. Jung*, 2d ed., vol. 8, trans. R. F. C. Hull (Princeton, N.J.: Princeton University Press, 1959); Jean Piaget, *The Origins of Intelligence in Children* (New York: International Universities Press, 1952); Heinz Werner, "The Concept of Development from a Comparative and Organismic Point of View," in *The Concept of Development: An Issue in the Study of Human Behavior*, ed. D. B. Harris, 125–48 (Minneapolis: University of Minnesota Press, 1957); Jane Loevinger, *Ego Development* (San Francisco, Calif.: Jossey-Bass, 1976).

6. See Polly Young-Eisendrath and James Hall, *Jung's Self Psychology: A Constructivist Perspective* (New York: Guilford Press, 1991).

7. For a discussion of Carl Jung's concept of empty center, see D. J. Meckel and R. L. Moore, eds., *Self and Liberation: The Jung/Buddhism Dialogue* (Mahwah, N.Y.: Paulist Press, 1992). In his later work, Jung talks about the self as an "empty center" or an underlying principle of organization: "The whole course of individuation is dialectical, and the so-called 'end' is the confrontation of the ego with the 'emptiness' of the centre. Here the limit of possible experience is reached; the ego dissolves as the reference point of cognition." Jung to a Swiss pastor, 1955; in C. G. Jung, *Letters, 1951–1961* (Princeton, N.J.: Princeton University Press, 1975), 2:259. The self is conceptualized as function also in Polly Young-Eisendrath and James A. Hall, "Ways of Speaking of Self," in *The Book of the Self: Person, Pretext, and Process*, ed. Polly Young-Eisendrath and James A. Hall (New York: New York University Press, 1987). For a discussion of Piaget's epistemic subject, see Jean Piaget, *Six Psychological Studies* (New York: Random House, 1967).

8. H. G. Gadamer, *Philosophical Hermeneutics* (Berkeley: University of California Press, 1977); H. G. Gadamer, *Truth and Method* (New York: Crossroads, 1982); Rom Harré, *Social Being* (Cambridge, Mass.: Blackwell, 1979); Rom Harré, *Personal Being: A Theory for Individual Psychol-*

ogy (Oxford, England: Basil Blackwell, 1983); Rom Harré, "The 'Self' as
a Theoretical Concept," in Relativism: Interpretation and Confrontation,
ed. M. Krausz (Notre Dame, Ind.: University of Notre Dame Press,
1989); M. Heidegger, Basic Concepts: 1889–1976, trans. G. E.
Aylesworth (Bloomington: University of Indiana Press, 1993); M. Heidegger, The Basic Problems of Phenomenology: 1889–1976, trans. A. Hofstadter (Bloomington: Indiana University Press, 1982); W. V. Quine,
Philosophy of Logic, 2d ed. (Cambridge, Mass.: Harvard University Press,
1986); W. V. Quine, The Philosophy of W. V. Quine, ed. L. E. Hahn and P.
A. Schilpp (La Salle, Ill.: Open Court, 1986); W. V. Quine, Pursuit of
Truth (Cambridge, Mass.: Harvard University Press, 1990); R. Rorty, The
Consequences of Pragmatism (Princeton, N.J.: Princeton University Press,
1982); R. Rorty, Contingency, Irony, and Solidarity (Cambridge, England:
Cambridge University Press, 1989); R. Rorty, "Inquiry as Recontextual-
ization: An Anti-Dualist Account of Interpretation," in The Interpretive
Turn: Philosophy, Science, Culture, ed. D. R. Hiley, J. F. Bohman, and R.
Shusterman (Ithaca, N.Y.: Cornell University Press, 1991), 59–80;
Charles Taylor, Human Agency and Language: Philosophical Papers, vol. 1
(Cambridge, England: Cambridge University Press, 1985); Charles Tay-
lor, Sources of the Self: The Making of the Modern Identity (Cambridge,
Mass.: Harvard University Press, 1989); L. Wittgenstein, Philosophical
Occasions: 1912–1951, ed. J. C. Klagge and A. Nordmann (Indianapolis,
Ind.: Hacket Publishing Co., 1993); L. Wittgenstein, The Wittgenstein
Reader: 1889–1951, ed. A. Kenny (Cambridge, Mass.: Blackwell, 1994);
Jane Flax, Disputed Subjects: Essays on Psychoanalysis, Politics and Philoso-
phy (New York: Routledge, 1993); Jane Flax, "Post-Modernism and
Gender Relations in Feminist Theory," Signs 12, no. 4 (1987): 621–43;
Jane Flax, "Remembering the Selves: Is the Repressed Gendered?" Michi-
gan Quarterly Review 26, no. 1 (1986): 92–110; Jane Flax, Thinking Frag-
ments: Psychoanalysis, Feminism, and Postmodernism in the Contemporary
West (Berkeley: University of California Press, 1990); S. Mitchell, Hope
and Dread in Psychoanalysis (New York: Basic Books, 1993); S. Mitchell,
Relational Concepts in Psychoanalysis: An Integration (Cambridge, Mass.:
Harvard University Press, 1984); Roy Schafer, Language and Insight (New
Haven, Conn.: Yale University Press, 1978); Roy Schafer, A New Language for Psychoanalysis (New Haven, Conn.: Yale University Press,
1976); Roy Schafer, Retelling a Life: Narration and Dialogue in Psychoanalysis (New York: Basic Books, 1992); Donald Spence, Narrative Truth,
Historical Truth (New York: W. W. Norton, 1982); Donald Spence, The

Freudian Metaphor: Toward Paradigm Change in Psychoanalysis (New York: W. W. Norton, 1987).

9. Polly Young-Eisendrath and Florence L. Wiedemann, *Female Authority: Empowering Women through Psychotherapy* (New York: Guilford Press, 1987); R. Seidenberg, "Psychoanalysis and Femininity," pt. 2, *Psychoanalytic Psychology* 8, no. 2 (1991): 225–37, esp. 227.

10. Essentialist theories assume that personality is founded principally from sources that arise outside of social influences, such as biology, genetics, basic organizing forms. Whether they are realist or idealist, essentialist theories assume causal explanations deriving from a context beyond human interpretation. From the perspective of postmodern critiques, essentialism is fundamentally in error because all knowledge is derived from human interpretations.

11. Young-Eisendrath and Hall, *Jung's Self Psychology*; Polly Young-Eisendrath, *You're Not What I Expected: Learning to Love the Opposite Sex* (New York: William Morrow, 1993); Polly Young-Eisendrath, "Gender and Individuation: Relating to Self and Other," in *Mirrors of Transformation: The Self in Relationships*, ed. D. E. Brien, 21–39 (Berwyn, Penn.: Round Table Press, 1995).

12. B. Beebe and Daniel Stern, "Engagement and Disengagement and Early Object Experiences," in *Communicative Structures and Psychic Structures*, ed. M. Freedman and S. Grand (New York: Plenum Press, 1977); B. Beebe and P. Sloate, "Assessment and Treatment of Difficulties in Mother-Infant Attunement in the First Three Years of Life: A Case History," *Psychoanalytic Inquiry* 1, no. 4 (1982): 601–23; J. D. Lichtenberg, "Implications for Psychoanalytic Theory of Research on the Neonate," *International Review of Psycho-Analysis* 8, no. 1 (1981): 35–52; J. D. Lichtenberg, *Psychoanalysis and Infant Research* (Hillsdale, N.J.: Analytic Press, 1983); J. D. Lichtenberg, "Mirrors and Mirroring: Developmental Experiences," *Psychoanalytic Inquiry* 5, no. 2 (1985): 199–210; J. D. Lichtenberg and D. G. Norton, *Cognitive and Mental Development in the First Five Years of Life: A Review of Recent Research* (Chevy Chase, Md.: National Institute of Mental Health, 1970); Daniel N. Stern, "Affect Attunement," in *Frontiers of Infant Psychiatry*, ed. J. D. Call, E. Galenson, and R. L. Tyson, vol. 2 (New York: Basic Books, 1985); Daniel N. Stern, *The Interpersonal World of the Infant* (New York: Basic Books, 1985).

13. C. E. Izard, *Human Emotions* (New York: Plenum Press, 1977); C. E. Izard, "Emotions as Motivations: An Evolutionary-Developmental Per-

spective," *Nebraska Symposium on Motivation* 26 (1978): 163–200; C. E. Izard, "Basic Emotions, Relations among Emotions, and Emotion-Cognition Relations," *Psychological Review* 99, no. 3 (1992): 561–65; C. E. Izard, "Innate and Universal Facial Expressions: Evidence from Developmental and Cross-Cultural Research," *Psychological Bulletin* 115, no. 2 (1994): 288–99; M. Lewis, "Self-Conscious Emotions and the Development of Self," *Journal of the American Psychoanalytic Association* 39, suppl. (1991): 45–73; M. Lewis and L. A. Rosenblum, *The Development of Affect* (New York: Plenum Press, 1978); S. S. Tompkins, *Affect, Imagery, and Consciousness*, vol. 1: *The Positive Affects* (New York: Springer, 1962); S. S. Tompkins, *Affect, Imagery, and Consciousness*, vol. 2: *The Negative Affects* (New York: Springer, 1963).

14. D. Goleman, *Emotional Intelligence* (New York: Bantam Books, 1995).

15. Jung, *Collected Works*, 18:518.

16. Goleman, *Emotional Intelligence*, 1995.

17. P. M. Roseneau, *Postmodernism and the Social Sciences: Insights, Inroads, and Intrusions* (Princeton, N.J.: Princeton University Press, 1992).

18. This branch of postmodernism values individual freedom and rejects all terms (such as *unity, connection, totality,* and *coherence*) that place constraints upon the process of knowing. While skeptical postmodernism values diversity and difference, I find that this diversity comes at the expense of connection, community, and unity. The affirmative branch of postmodernism, on the other hand, argues that community and diversity complement each other. For critiques of skeptical postmodernism, see Overton, "Arrow of Time and Cycle of Time"; and Charles Taylor, *The Ethics of Authenticity* (Cambridge, Mass.: Harvard University Press, 1992).

19. J. Derrida, "How to Avoid Speaking: Denials," in *Derrida and Negation Theology*, ed. K. Frieden (Albany, N.Y.: SUNY Press, 1974); J. Derrida, *Positions*, trans. A. Bass (Chicago: University of Chicago Press, 1981); J. Derrida, "Différance," in *Margins of Philosophy*, by J. Derrida, trans. A. Bass (Chicago: University of Chicago Press, 1982); J. Derrida, *The Post Card: From Socrates to Freud and Beyond*, trans. A. Bass (Chicago: University of Chicago Press, 1987); J. Derrida, *Given Time*, trans. P. Kamuf (Chicago: University of Chicago Press, 1992).

20. Charles Taylor, *Philosophical Arguments* (Cambridge, Mass.: Harvard University Press, 1995), 62.

21. N. Tinbergen, *The Study of Instinct* (London: Oxford University Press, 1951).

22. Jung, *Collected Works*, vol. 9, sec. 1. For a full treatment of the evolution of the term *archetype* in Jung's work, see Young-Eisendrath and Hall,

Jung's Self Psychology. The definition of *archetype* used in the present volume resonates with Jung's work on the concept after 1945. He changed what initially had been an essentialist Kantian concept of "mental image" into something akin to an "innate releasing mechanism" in evolutionary biology. Jung's later definition refers to a predisposition for specific images to *cohere* in emotionally aroused states. Human beings universally are "prewired" to form emotionally charged images of the Great Mother and Terrible Mother, no matter what their specific cultures may be. Archetypes are familiar the world over because they derive from common human emotions that we all share and from ubiquitous conditions of human life, such as the stages of the lifespan. Early archetypal images first cohere in states of powerful emotion during our powerless infancy. Later in life, they continue to affect us in predictable ways. When we are living out an archetype, rather than sensing it as emanating from our own attitudes and perceptions, we are captured by primitive states (ranging from idealized love to terror) that can be extremely distressing.

23. For a review of Jung's theory of psychological complexes, see C. G. Jung, "A Review of the Complex Theory," in Jung, *Collected Works*, vol. 8, 92–104. Also see Jung, *Collected Works*, vol. 2, 598–603. Jung's later theory of complexes included the idea that *every* complex is characterized by an emotional state that emanates from a core archetypal image. The complex itself is a collection of associated bits of experience (e.g., ideas, habits, sensations) that cohere around an emotional core. A complex becomes a subpersonality of the unconscious when it is enacted or experienced repeatedly.

24. Goleman, *Emotional Intelligence*.

25. Young-Eisendrath, *You're Not What I Expected*, details how our complexes, formed in early experiences with primary caregivers, later manifest themselves in relationships with romantic partners.

26. C. G. Jung, "Psychological Commentary on *The Tibetan Book of the Great Liberation*" (1939) in Meckel and Moore, eds., *Self and Liberation*, 50.

Chapter 2.
Gender, Constrasexuality, and Self

1. Within hours of a child's birth, adults already have gender expectations for their children. In one study, parents were asked to describe their twenty-four-hour-old baby. Even though these newborns were equivalent in measures of length, weight, and robustness, parents of boys and girls

provided different characterizations. Parents of a son were more likely to describe their newborn as big, large-featured, and attentive; parents of daughters used descriptors such as soft, little, beautiful, delicate, fine-featured, and inattentive. J. Z. Rubin, F. J. Provenzano, and Z. Luria, "The Eye of the Beholder: Parents' Views on Sex of Newborns," *American Journal of Orthopsychiatry* 43 (1974): 720–31.

In another study, three-month-olds were dressed in both male and female clothes on two separate occasions. Adults were not told an infant's sex but were asked to describe the baby. Adults rated infants in female clothes as round, soft, fragile, and more fearful. When the same infants were dressed in male clothes, they were perceived as strong, angry, and sturdy. C. A. Seavey, P. A. Katz, and S. R. Zalk, "Baby X: The Effect of Gender Labels on Adult Responses to Infant," *Sex Roles* 1 (1975): 103–10.

Research suggests that adults also express their gender expectations in the early years by purchasing and encouraging their infants to play with gender-appropriate toys. See, e.g., T. D. Fisher, "Adult Toy Purchases for Children: Factors Affecting Sex-Typed Toy Selection," *Journal of Applied Developmental Psychology* 14, no. 3 (1993): 385–406. Parents engage their toddlers in gender-appropriate play; for example, fathers and sons engage in play which centers around vehicles and tools, whereas the play of fathers and daughters revolves around domestic themes. J. Farver and S. Wimbarti, "Paternal Participation in Toddlers' Pretend Play," *Social Development* 4, no. 1 (1995): 17–31. This indoctrination is so prevalent that, at a very young age, children prefer and, indeed, expect other children to choose gender-consistent toys. C. L. Martin, L. Eisenbud, and H. Rose, "Children's Gender-Based Reasoning about Toys," *Child Development* 66, no. 5 (1995): 1453–72. Also see K. MacDonald and R. Parke, "Parent-Child Physical Play: The Effects of Sex and Age of Children and Parents," *Sex Roles* 15 (1986): 367–78; Judy Mann, *The Difference: Growing Up Female in America* (New York: Warner Books, 1994); L. A. Roggman and J. C. Peery, "Parent-Infant Social Play in Brief Encounters: Early Gender Differences," *Child Study Journal* 19, no. 1 (1989): 65–79.

2. Several researchers have presented evidence that the brain pathways determining behavior differ in some ways in males and females, due to chromosomal and hormonal differences produced in each sex. A. A. Ehrhardt and H. F. L. Meyer-Bahlburg, "Effects of Prenatal Sex Hormones on Gender-Related Behavior," *Science* 211 (1981): 1312–18; and N. J. MacLusky and F. Naftolin, "Sexual Differentiation of the Central

Nervous System," *Science* 211 (1981): 1294–1303. Jerome Bruner, however, argues compellingly in *Acts of Meaning* (Cambridge, Mass.: Harvard University Press, 1990) that, while biological structure may impose "constraints on action[,] . . . it is culture, not biology, that shapes human life and the human mind" (p. 34).

3. P. R. Sanday, *Female Power and Male Dominance: On the Origins of Sexual Inequality* (Cambridge, England: Cambridge University Press, 1981).

4. Mary Catherine Bateson, *Peripheral Visions: Learning Along the Way* (New York: Harper Collins, 1994).

5. Particularly destructive is the patriarchal expectation that women will be more dependent and less competent than healthy adults. Research indicates that the descriptions given by many trained clinicians of a "healthy adult male" and a "healthy adult, sex unspecified" were identical. These descriptions included strength, objectivity, competence and independence. When asked to describe the "healthy adult female," the same respondents suggested greater weakness, less competence, more emotional expression, and greater subjectivity than was expected from either a "healthy male" or a "healthy adult." Thus, if women behave like healthy adults, they are seen as unwomanly, but if they behave as a woman is expected to behave, they are seen as inferior to "healthy adults." I. K. Broverman, D. M. Broverman, F. E. Clarkson, P. S. Rosenkrantz, and S. R. Vogel, "Sex-Role Stereotypes and Clinical Judgments of Mental Health," *Journal of Consulting and Clinical Psychology* 34 (1970): 1–7; I. K. Broverman, S. R. Vogel, D. M. Broverman, F. E. Clarkson, and P. S. Rosenkrantz, "Sex-Role Stereotypes: A Current Appraisal," *Journal of Social Issues* 28 (1972): 59–78; G. Baruch and R. Barnett, "Role Quality, Multiple Role Involvement, and Psychological Well-Being in Midlife Women," *Journal of Personality and Social Psychology* 51 (1986): 578–85.

6. As of 1988, women with a college degree still were earning only 59 cents for every dollar earned by a man of the same or considerably less education. For a review of the relevant statistics, see S. Faludi, *Backlash: The Undeclared War Against American Women* (New York: Crown, 1991), ch. 13; B. Wagman and N. Folbre, "The Feminization of Inequality: Some New Patterns," *Challenge* 31, no. 6 (1988): 56–59.

7. Statistic from *Mediamark Research Multimedia Audience Report*, Spring 1990 (New York: Mediamark Research, Inc., 1990).

8. John Money and A. A. Ehrhardt, *Man and Woman, Boy and Girl: The Differentiation and Dimorphism of Gender Identity from Conception to Maturity* (Baltimore, Md.: Johns Hopkins University Press, 1972).

9. Carol Tavris, *The Mismeasure of Woman* (New York: Simon and Schuster, 1992).

10. Schafer, *Retelling a Life*, 68.

11. Jung believed that men, universally and biologically, were the natural "cultural makers"—more objective, better leaders, more rational, more independent. He believed that women, universally and biologically, were the "relaters," better at caring for others, knowing their feelings and emotions, and valuing relationships. Freud believed that women were "inferior men," missing certain aspects of intelligence and morality endowed in the male biological makeup. In contrast, Jung believed that women and men were designed to "specialize" in different, but equally valuable, functions.

12. Demaris S. Wehr, *Jung and Feminism: Liberating Archetypes* (Boston: Beacon Press, 1987); Young-Eisendrath and Wiedemann, *Female Authority*; Mary Ann Mattoon and Jennifer Jones, "Is the Animus Obsolete?" *Quadrant* 20, no. 1 (1987): 5–22; Andrew Samuels, *The Plural Psyche: Personality, Morality, and the Father* (London: Routledge, 1989); Claire Douglas, *The Woman in the Mirror: Analytic Psychology and the Feminine* (Boston, Mass.: Sigo Press, 1990); Deldon McNeely, *Women and the Trickster* (Woodstock, Conn.: Spring Publications, 1996); and Young-Eisendrath, *You're Not What I Expected*.

13. The stereotype that women are more emotional has received some empirical support. Research on emotional expressiveness generally has found that women express sadness, love, and happiness more than men. In one study of 100 male and 125 female college students, self-rated expressions of fear and sadness, and the level of confidence in the ability to express these emotions, were significantly higher for women than for men. See O. J. Balswick, *The Inexpressive Male* (Lexington, Mass.: Lexington Books, 1988); and M. J. Blier and L. A. Blier-Wilson, "Gender Differences in Self-Rated Emotional Expressiveness," *Sex Roles* 2, nos. 3 and 4 (1989): 287–95.

The assumption that women are more empathic and relationally oriented has found support, too. In 1983, N. Eisenberg and R. Lennon reviewed over a hundred studies of gender differences in empathy and concluded that there is a "huge sex difference in self-report of empathy [women reported themselves more empathic] as measured with questionnaires." However, when heart rates or videotaped facial reactions were analyzed, no consistent sex differences were found. These findings suggest that women are more likely than men to report themselves as empathic and that men may experience similar empathy but express it less. Nancy Eisenberg and R. Lennon, "Sex Differences in Empathy and Related Capacities," *Psychological Bulletin* 94 (1983): 100–131.

14. Jung's theory of contrasexuality posits the development of an opposite-sex personality which may become manifest in the second half of life when some of us confront our unconscious projections of Otherness and begin to sense the Other in ourselves. For Jung's theory of contrasexuality and development, see C. G. Jung, "Aion," in Jung, *Collected Works*, vol. 9; and "Anima and Animus," in Jung, *Collected Works*, vol. 7. Jung's notion that everyone has a biologically based opposite-sex personality, linked to genetic (hormonal, morphological, etc.) traces of the other sex, is "essentialist." Whereas Jung believed that gender differences are determined biologically, I believe that gender (in all its ramifications) is relatively flexible and dependent on context and culture. Polly Young-Eisendrath, "Rethinking Feminism, the Animus, and the Feminine," in *To Be a Woman*, ed. C. Zweig (Los Angeles, Calif.: Tarcher, 1990); and Polly Young-Eisendrath, "Gender, Animus, and Related Topics," in *Gender and Soul in Psychotherapy*, ed. Nathan Schwart-Salant and M. Stein (Wilmette, Ill.: Chiron, 1991).

15. See Sigmund Freud, "Some Psychical Consequences of the Anatomical Distinction between the Sexes," in Sigmund Freud, *The Standard Edition of the Complete Works of Sigmund Freud*, ed. J. Strachey, vol. 19 (1925; reprint, London: Hogarth Press, 1961).

16. Jacqueline Rose, "Introduction—II," in *Feminine Sexuality: Jacques Lacan and the Ecole Freudienne*, ed. Juliet Mitchell and Jacqueline Rose, trans. Jacqueline Rose (New York: W. W. Norton, 1982), 33.

17. Young-Eisendrath, *You're Not What I Expected*; Polly Young-Eisendrath, *The Gifts of Suffering: Finding Insight, Compassion, and Renewal* (Reading, Mass.: Addison-Wesley, 1996); Young-Eisendrath and Wiedemann, *Female Authority*.

18. E. E. Maccoby, "Gender and Relationships: A Developmental Account," *American Psychologist* 45, no. 4 (1990): 513–20; E. E. Maccoby, "Gender and Relationships: A Reprise," *American Psychologist* 46, no. 5 (1991): 538–39; Rhoda Unger, *Representations: Social Constructions of Gender* (Los Gatos, Calif.: Baywood Publishers, 1989), 22.

19. Maccoby, "Gender and Relationships: A Developmental Account."

20. For early major critiques of applying theories of male development to female development, see Carol Gilligan, "Woman's Place in Man's Life Cycle," *Harvard Educational Review* 49, no. 4 (1979): 431–46; and Carol

Gilligan, *In a Different Voice: Psychological Theory and Women's Development* (Cambridge, Mass.: Harvard University Press, 1982).

21. Schafer, *Retelling a Life,* 76.

22. Young-Eisendrath, *You're Not What I Expected,* 23–27.

23. Two-year-olds can identify the sex of people in pictures, and normally three-year-olds refer to themselves as either boys or girls. The results of one of these studies suggested that twenty-six-month-olds were significantly more likely to demonstrate gender labeling, gender identity, preference for appropriate sex-typed toys, and awareness of adult sex-role differences than would be expected by chance. It is not until approximately age six or seven, however, that most children understand that gender is an enduring feature of another person and of themselves (gender constancy). Lawrence Kohlberg argued that children learn about gender roles the same way they learn about any other concept. Once children have learned how to classify the world into male and female, they actively structure their world into male and female segments and act in accord with the gender roles "appropriate" for their sex. Lawrence Kohlberg, "A Cognitive Developmental Analysis of Children's Sex-Role Concepts and Attitudes," in *The Development of Sex Differences*, ed. E. E. Maccoby (Stanford, Calif.: Stanford University Press, 1966); John Money, "Differentiation of Gender Identity," *JSAS Catalog of Selected Documents in Psychology* 6, no. 4 (1976):; D. Ruble, "Sex-Role Development," in *Development Psychology: An Advanced Textbook*, ed. M. H. Bornstein and M. E. Lamb (Hillsdale, N.J.: Lawrence Erlbaum, 1983). M. Weinraub, L. P. Clemens, A. Sockloff, T. Ethridge, E. Gracely, and B. Myers, "The Development of Sex-Role Stereotypes in the Third Year: Relationships to Gender Labeling, Gender Identity, Sex-Typed Toy Preference, and Family Characteristics," *Child Development* 55 (1984): 1493–1503.

24. In one study, boys received significantly more condemnation than girls for crossing gender lines, and fathers were much more strict than mothers in seeing that their male child adhered to sex-appropriate behavior. See B. I. Fagot and R. Hagan, "Observations of Parent Reactions to Sex-Stereotyped Behaviors: Age and Sex Effects," *Child Development* 62, no. 3 (1991): 617–28; C. N. Jacklin, J. A. DiPietro, and E. E. Maccoby, "Sex-Typing Behavior and Sex-Typing Pressure in Child-Parent Interaction," *Archives of Sexual Behavior* 13, no. 5 (1985): 413–25; M. E. Snow, C. N. Jacklin, and E. E. Maccoby, "Sex-of-Child Differences in Father-Child Interaction at One Year of Age," *Child Development* 54, no. 1 (1983):

227–32. The greater condemnation of boys may explain why recent studies find that males act more strongly sex-typed than females. T. L. Pellett and J. M. Harrison, "Children's Perceptions of the Gender Appropriateness of Physical Activities: A Further Analysis," *Play and Culture* 5, no. 3 (1992): 305–13; H. Trautner, "Boys' and Girls' Play Behavior in Same-Sex and Opposite-Sex Pairs," *Journal of Genetic Psychology* 156 (1995): 5–15.

25. Myra Sadker and David Sadker cite two studies, one they themselves conducted and another involving 1,100 twelve-year-olds from the Michigan school system. Sixth-graders were asked to write descriptions of what they would do if they woke up one day and found themselves members of the opposite sex. Females tended to welcome the change, whereas boys were appalled by the idea. In the Michigan study, 42 percent of the girls felt the change would be positive, while only 5 percent of the boys felt this way. In fact, boys imagined creative ways to escape "such a terrible fate." In both studies, some boys even claimed they would have to kill themselves. Myra Sadker and David Sadker, *Failing at Fairness: How America's Schools Cheat Girls* (New York: Macmillan, 1994).

26. There is extensive empirical evidence demonstrating gender segregation in children's play groups. T. Daniels-Beirness, "Measuring Peer Status in Boys and Girls: A Problem of Apples and Oranges," in *Social Competence in Developmental Perspective*, 2d ed., ed. B. H. Schneider, G. Attili, J. Nadel, and R. P. Weissberg (Boston, Mass.: Kluwer Academic Publishers, 1989); C. Feiring and M. Lewis, "The Child's Social Network: Sex Differences from Three to Six Years," *Sex Roles* 17 (1987): 621–36; C. N. Jacklin and E. E. Maccoby, "Social Behavior at Thirty-Three Months in Same-Sex and Mixed-Sex Dyads," *Child Development* 49, no. 3 (1978): 557–69; and E. E. Maccoby, "Gender as a Social Category," *Developmental Psychology* 24, no. 6 (1988): 755–65. Even in early adolescence, when the sexes begin to take a romantic interest in one another, adolescents typically socialize in mixed-gender groups; in early to middle adolescence, dating is more a "group project" than two individuals spending time alone together. It is not until later in high school that romantic dyads begin to become more common. M. Cole and S. R. Cole, *The Development of Children*, 2d ed. (New York: Scientific American Books, 1993), ch. 5.

27. Melanie Klein, *Envy and Gratitude and Other Works* (New York: Free Press, 1975).

28. Studies have found that women are significantly more likely to see doctors about physical complaints; see, e.g., J. Mirowsky and C. E. Ross, "Sex

Differences in Distress: Real or Artifact?" *American Sociological Review* 60, no. 3 (1995): 449–68. They also are much more likely to use mental health services; see N. F. Russo, "Forging Research Priorities for Women's Mental Health," *American Psychologist* 45, no. 3 (1990): 368–73. For discussions of women's greater longevity, see W. R. Hazzard, "Biological Basis of the Sex Differential in Longevity," *Journal of the American Geriatrics Society* 34, no. 6 (1986): 455–71; and L. M. Verbrugge, "Gender and Health: An Update on Hypotheses and Evidence," *Journal of Health and Social Behavior* 26, no. 3 (1985): 156–82.

29. While mothers have been idealized throughout history, actual mothers have received very little prestige and respect. A. Dally, *Inventing Motherhood: The Consequences of an Ideal* (New York: Schocken Books, 1982); and Adrienne Rich, *Of Woman Born: Motherhood as Experience and Institution* (New York: W. W. Norton, 1976).

30. Use of Dialogue Therapy with couples is described in Polly Young-Eisendrath, *Hags and Heroes: A Feminist Approach to Jungian Psychotherapy with Couples* (Toronto, Canada: Inner City Books, 1984); Young-Eisendrath, *You're Not What I Expected.*

31. Carl Jung, (1951), in Jung, *Collected Works,* 9; "Anima and Animus," 11–22.

32. Ibid., 9:13.

33. Ibid., 9:15.

34. A number of studies have found that girls, despite equivalent achievement test scores and grades, provide lower estimations of their performance and competence and attribute their successes to hard work or luck instead of ability. Boys, on the other hand, overestimate their performances and attribute their successes to their ability and intelligence. This finding held true even for early adolescent males and females who scored at or above the 98th percentile on a math aptitude test. V. J. Crandall, "Sex Differences in Expectancy of Intellectual and Academic Performance," in *Women: Dependent or Independent Variable?,* ed. Rhoda Unger and F. Denmark (New York: Psychological Dimensions, 1975), 649–85; C. Dweck et al., "Sex Differences in Learned Helplessness: II. The Contingencies of Evaluative Feedback in the Classroom; and III. An Experimental Analysis," *Developmental Psychology* 14 (1978): 268–76; E. Fennema and G. Leder, *Mathematics and Gender* (New York: Teachers College Press, Columbia University, 1990); L. Kramer, "Gifted Adolescent Girls: Self-Perceptions of Ability within One Middle School Setting" (Ph.D. diss., University of Florida, 1985); D. J. Stipek, "Sex

Differences in Children's Attributions for Success and Failure on Math and Spelling Tests," *Sex Roles* 11 (1984): 969–81; D. K. Yee and J. S. Eccles, "Parent Perceptions and Attributions for Children's Math Achievement," *Sex Roles* 19 (1988): 317–33. For an excellent popular discussion of the origins and consequences of this gender difference in ability estimations, see Mann, *The Difference*. Gender differences in self-estimation carry over into adulthood. Rosalind C. Barnett and Grace K. Baruch, in *The Competent Woman: Perspectives on Development* (New York: Irvington Publishers, 1978), review some of the research on this interesting gender difference. They cite one large-scale study of senior college students, in which the male students with C+ averages believed themselves competent to earn the Ph.D. degree. The women in this study with B+ or better averages did not see themselves as competent to obtain this advanced degree. More recent research also finds that males give higher IQ estimates to themselves than to females, and that both sexes provide higher estimates for father's IQ than for mother's IQ. A. Furnham and R. Rawles, "Sex Differences in the Estimation of Intelligence," *Journal of Social Behavior and Personality* 10, no. 3 (1995): 741–48; N. Hamid and D. Lok, "Gender Stereotyping in Estimates of Intelligence in Chinese Students," *Journal of Social Psychology* 135, no. 3 (1995): 407–409.

35. For a description of a nationwide poll assessing self-esteem, educational experiences, interest in math and science, and career aspirations of girls and boys aged 9–15, see American Association of University Women, *Shortchanging Girls, Shortchanging America* (Washington, D.C.: Green-berg-Lake, 1991). A substantial number of studies have demonstrated that girls' self-esteem and confidence decline significantly across the middle school years, as compared to those of boys. B. Allgood-Merten, P. Lewinsohn, and H. Hops, "Sex Differences and Adolescent Depression," *Journal of Abnormal Psychology* 91, no. 1 (1990): 55–63; B. Herman, "Changing Sources of Self-Esteem among Boys and Girls in Secondary Schools," *Urban Education* 24 (1990): 432–39; B. E. Kline and E. B. Short, "Changes in Emotional Resilience: Gifted Adolescent Females," *Roeper Review* 13, no. 3 (1991): 118–21, P. B. Moran and J. Eckenrode, "Gender Differences in the Costs and Benefits of Peer Relationships during Adolescence," *Journal of Adolescent Research* 6, no. 4 (1991): 396–409.

36. The different treatment given boys and girls in the classroom encourages assertiveness in boys and passivity in girls. Boys receive more criticism, are asked more challenging questions, and are given more instruction. As

a result, boys learn that they are important and competent, and they are taught to sharpen their ideas, find their voices, and achieve more. Girls, on the other hand, by being ignored, learn that they should be quiet, defer to males, and relinquish their ambitions. Research by Myra Sadker and David Sadker suggests that the greater attention allotted to males occurs regardless of the ratio of boys to girls in a classroom and regardless of the teacher's sex. The Sadkers found that this preferential treatment begins in the elementary school years and continues into college. Myra Sadker and David Sadker, *Year 3: Final Report: Promoting Effectiveness in Classroom Instruction* (Washington, D.C.: National Institute for Education, 1984); Myra Sadker and David Sadker, "Sexism in the Classroom: From Grade School to Graduate School," *Phi Delta Kappan* 67 (1986): 512–15; G. Leinhardt, A. Seewald, and M. Engel, "Learning What's Taught: Sex Differences in Instruction," *Journal of Educational Psychology* 71 (1979): 432–39; L. C. Wilkinson and C. Marrett, eds., *Gender Influences in Classroom Interaction* (Orlando, Fla.: Academic Press, 1985). For a very accessible and complete summation of the Sadkers' research, see Myra Sadker and David Sadker, *Failing at Fairness.*

The preferential treatment given to males has been documented in other studies of the college classroom. Catherine Krupnick concluded from her studies of Harvard University classrooms that the men performed and the women watched. See her "Unlearning Gender Roles," in *Gender and Public Policy: Cases and Comments*, ed. K. Winston and M. Bane (Boulder, Colo.: Westview Press, 1992). Other studies have found that professors remember male students' names more often and call on and listen to males more than females. B. Sandler and R. Hall, *The Classroom Climate: A Chilly One for Women* (Washington, D.C.: Association of American Colleges, 1982).

37. The empirical literature suggests that adolescent females sacrifice their academic achievement for the sake of popularity. Beginning in the middle school years, appearance and popularity are the attributes most valued in a female. Detailing the results of her study, Anne Petersen reported that, in seventh grade, females who had the poorest body image and the most depressive symptoms were the most academically successful girls. Of this group of girls, a year later, the girls who had improved in terms of depression and self-image were those who had *lowered* their academic achievement. This pattern persisted into twelfth grade! Girls learned to sacrifice achievement and assertiveness—long-term success— for a short-term gratification—popularity. Anne Petersen, "The Gangly

Years," *Psychology Today*, Sept. 1987, pp. 28–34; G. R. Adams and J. L. Roopnarine, "Physical Attractiveness, Social Skills, and Same-Sex Peer Popularity," *Journal of Group Psychotherapy, Psychodrama, and Sociometry* 47 (1994): 15–35; J. Coleman, *The Adolescent Society* (New York: Free Press, 1961); and Kramer, *Gifted Adolescent Girls*.

Other researchers, too, have found that what makes a girl popular are being "cute" or "pretty," wearing the right clothes, "bubbly" personality, and being a cheerleader or a friend of one. Not on this list are the qualities of independence, courage, creativity, honesty, achievement, and intelligence. Thus, the message girls receive is that brains are a barrier to popularity. One study indicated that teachers readily could pick out intelligent males but were surprised to discover which females were intelligent; this finding suggests that intelligent girls learn to hide their intelligence. Myra Sadker and David Sadker, *Failing at Fairness*.

38. L. M. Brown and Carol Gilligan, *Meeting at the Crossroads: Women's Psychology and Girl's Development* (Cambridge, Mass.: Harvard University Press, 1992); Carol Gilligan, "The Centrality of Relationship in Human Development" (paper presented at the Symposium of the Jean Piaget Society, Montreal, Quebec, Canada, May 1992); Carol Gilligan, "Women's Psychological Development: Implications for Psychotherapy," in *Women, Girls, and Psychotherapy: Reframing Resistance*, ed. Carol Gilligan, G. Rogers, and D. L. Tolman, 5–31 (Binghamton, N.Y.: Harrington Park Press, 1991).

39. Empirical studies consistently suggest that women experience significantly more depression than men. W. W. Eaton and L. G. Kessler, *Epidemiologic Field Methods in Psychiatry: The NIMH Epidemiologic Catchment Area Program* (Orlando, Fla.: Academic Press, 1985); Kline and Short, "Changes in Emotional Resilience"; P. M. Lewinsohn et al., "Adolescent Psychopathology: II. Psychosocial Risk Factors for Depression," *Journal of Abnormal Psychology* 103, no. 2 (1994): 302–15; S. Nolen-Hoeksema, "Sex Differences in Unipolar Depression: Evidence and Theory," *Psychological Bulletin* 101, no. 2 (1987): 259–82; M. M. Weissman and G. L. Klerman, "Sex Differences and the Epidemiology of Depression," *Archives of General Psychiatry* 34 (1977): 98–111. This significant gender difference in rates of depression emerges sometime during the adolescent years. Allgood-Merten, Lewinsohn, and Hops, "Sex Differences and Adolescent Depression," 55–63; S. Nolen-Hoeksema and J. S. Girgus, "The Emergence of Gender Differences in Depression during Adolescence," *Psychological Bulletin* 115, no. 3 (1994): 424–43; Anne C. Pe-

tersen, P. A. Sarigiani, and R. E. Kennedy, "Adolescent Depression: Why More Girls?" *Journal of Youth and Adolescence* 20, no. 2 (1991): 247–71.

Clinician Harriet Goldhor Lerner, "Female Depression: Self-Sacrifice and Self-Betrayal in Relationships," in *Depression and Women: A Lifespan Perspective*, ed. R. Formanek and A. Gurian (New York: Springer Publishing Co., 1987), p. 200, speculates that female depression may be linked to an excessive self-sacrifice that occurs when "too much of the self (one's beliefs, convictions, wants, priorities, ambitions) become negotiable under relationship pressures." This process of "de-selfing" originates in women's childhood relationships as a defense against object loss and is reinforced in adult heterosexual relationships. Dana Jack, also from a relational perspective, proposes that when women attempt to fit the role of "self-sacrificing and ever caring woman," they become susceptible to self-alienation, inauthenticity, and consequent depression. Dana Jack, "Silencing the Self: The Power of Social Imperatives in Female Depression," in *Depression and Women: A Lifespan Perspective*, ed. R. Formanek and A. Gurian (New York: Springer Publishing Co., 1987).

Male-female differences in self-esteem may be a reason why men feel free to interrupt women. For a review of current research on interrupting behavior and gender styles of communicating, see D. Tannen, *You Just Don't Understand: Women and Men in Conversation* (New York: William Morrow, 1990), 188–215.

40. In midlife, women often are freed from their responsibilities to others and find in themselves great strength and satisfaction. For many, high accomplishments begin only after this freedom is obtained. Carolyn G. Heilbrun, *Hamlet's Mother and Other Women* (New York: Columbia University Press, 1990). Boys, on the other hand, typically are encouraged to pursue unrealistically high career aspirations. When these are not fulfilled later in life, chronic feelings of failure and disappointment can result. M. Komarovsky, *Dilemmas of Masculinity: A Study of College Youth* (New York: W. W. Norton, 1976); J. Pleck and R. Brannon, "Male Roles and the Male Experience," *Journal of Social Issues* 34 (1978): 1–4. While males have certain advantages, it is questionable whether their socialization is, in the long run, constructive. A number of statistics demonstrate that older males are exposed to, and are victims of, various forms of violence, at rates alarmingly higher than those for females. Consider the following sample of statistics. Males are three times more likely than

females to become alcohol dependent and 50 percent more likely to use illicit drugs. Men account for more than 90 percent of alcohol- and drug-related arrests. W. D. Watts and L. S. Wright, "The Relationship of Alcohol, Tobacco, Marijuana, and Other Illegal Drug Use to Delinquency Among Mexican-American, Black, and White Adolescent Males," *Adolescence* 25 (1990): 171–81. Males' recklessness also is apparent in auto accident rates. The leading cause of death among white males fifteen to twenty-four years old is auto accidents. See Children's Defense Fund, *The State of America's Children: 1992* (Washington, D.C.: Children's Defense Fund, 1992). Females may attempt suicide more often than males, but males "successfully" complete suicide significantly (three to four times) more often than females, and their methods are more violent than those of females. D. Lester, *Why People Kill Themselves: A 1990s Summary of Research Findings on Suicide Behavior* (Springfield, Ill.: Charles C. Thompson, 1992).

41. We constantly are bombarded with these gender stories. The lower value and second-class status of women in our society are evident in the media. Empirical studies of media content have shown that males are depicted as powerful and capable engineers, heroes, and villains; while females are presented either as supporters or as impediments to men's endeavors, being relegated to the sidelines or even rendered invisible. R. S. Craig, "The Effect of Television Day Part on Gender Portrayals in Television Commercials: A Content Analysis," *Sex Roles* 26 (1992): 197–211; S. Faludi, *Backlash*, ch. 4; Mann, *The Difference*, ch. 4; L. R. Vande Berg and D. Streckfuss, "Prime-Time Television's Portrayal of Women and the World of Work: A Demographic Profile," *Journal of Broadcasting and Electronic Media* 36, no. 2 (1992): 195–208. Numerous content analyses of textbooks have concluded that women are conspicuously absent from textbooks. In fact, in a 631-page "non-sexist" history text, only 7 pages were dedicated to women, and there was no reference to Susan B. Anthony. See Myra Sadker and David Sadker, *Failing at Fairness*, ch. 3.

42. See pp. 53–56, in this volume, for a discussion of this topic.

43. Our society's hypervaluation of autonomy is discussed by many feminist theorists of psychology, anthropology, literature, and theology. A recent interesting account comes from a Buddhist scholar, Ann Klein, *Meeting the Great Bliss Queen: Buddhists, Feminists, and the Art of the Self* (Boston, Mass.: Beacon Press, 1994). Also see Gilligan, "Woman's Place in Man's Life Cycle"; Gilligan, *In a Different Voice*; S. Harding, *Whose Science,*

Whose Knowledge: Thinking from Women's Lives (Ithaca, N.Y.: Cornell University Press, 1991); Harré, *Social Being*; Harré, *Personal Being*; J. V. Jordan, A. Kaplan, J. B. Miller, I. Stiver, and J. Surrey, *Women's Growth in Connection: Writings from the Stone Center* (New York: Guilford Press, 1991).

44. Jung believed that movement toward unity throughout life is a problem which is never solved. C. G. Jung, "Psychological Types," in Jung, *Collected Works*, 6:460. A similar "Buddhist" perspective is evident in Jung's work when he suggests why analysis cannot be a final "cure": "Life has always to be tackled anew . . . The new attitude gained in the course of analysis tends sooner or later to become inadequate in one way or another, and *necessarily* so, because the *constant flow* of life again and again demands fresh adaptation." Jung, "The Transcendent Function," *Collected Works*, 8:72–73. Also see ch. 1, n. 8, above, on the "empty center."

45. John Beebe, *Integrity in Depth* (College Station: Texas A&M University Press, 1992.)

46. For examples of theorists who conceive of the self as a construction and as emerging from a relational matrix, see W. R. D. Fairbairn, *An Object-Relations Theory of the Personality* (New York: Basic Books, 1952); T. H. Ogden, *The Matrix of the Mind: Object Relations and the Psychoanalytic Dialogue* (Northvale, N.J.: Jason Aronson, 1986); Overton, "Arrow of Time and Cycle of Time," 215–37; Harry Stack Sullivan, *The Interpersonal Theory of Psychiatry* (New York: W. W. Norton, 1953); Charles Taylor, *Sources of the Self*; Charles Taylor, "The Dialogical Self," in *The Interpretive Turn: Philosophy, Science, Culture*, ed. D. R. Hiley, J. F. Bohman, and R. Shusterman (Ithaca, N.Y.: Cornell University Press, 1991). For a discussion of variations of self across cultures and the reflection of these in language, see Harré, *Social Being*; and Harré, *Personal Being*.

47. Harré, *Personal Being*; J. MacMurray, *The Form of the Personal*, 2 vols. (London: Faber and Faber, 1957 and 1961); P. F. Strawson, *Individuals: An Essay in Descriptive Metaphysics* (London: Methuen, 1959); Charles Taylor, *Sources of the Self*.

48. Huston Smith, introduction to P. Kapleau, *The Three Pillars of Zen* (New York: Doubleday, 1965), p. xi. David Rosen has informed me that, in the specifics of this matter, Marie-Louise von Franz, in conversation with Rosen, said that Jung read this book fully several weeks before he died and that she possesses the actual text with Jung's notations in it.

49. Carl Jung "Introduction to D.T. Suzuki's *Introduction to Zen Buddhism*" (1939), cited in Meckel and Moore, eds., *Self and Liberation*.

50. In using Buddhism as a context, I do not mean to suggest that other spiritual or scientific contexts are not equally helpful for understanding Jung's concepts. Indeed, a Christian context most often is used in exploring the spiritual side of Jung's work. Rather, I want to show how useful Buddhism can be in illuminating a postmodern view of Jung's theory of the Self and the ego complex.

51. The following texts provide an overview of Buddhist philosophy for the uninitiated. Dalai-Lama, *A Policy of Kindness* (Ithaca, N.Y.: Snow Lion Publications, 1990); J. Goldstein and J. Kornfield, *Seeking the Heart of Wisdom: The Path of Insight Meditation* (Boston, Mass.: Shambhala, 1987); P. Kapleau, *Three Pillars of Zen*; J. Kornfield, *A Path with Heart: A Guide Through the Perils and Promises of Spiritual Life* (New York: Bantam Books, 1993); W. Rahula, *What the Buddha Taught* (New York: Grove Press, 1959); S. Suzuki, *Zen Mind, Beginner's Mind*, ed. T. Dixon (New York: Weatherhill, 1970).

52. Rahula, *What the Buddha Taught*, 51.

53. Psychiatrist Mark Epstein, in his recent book about Buddhism and psychoanalysis, *Thoughts Without a Thinker: Psychotherapy from a Buddhist Perspective* (New York: Basic Books, 1995), puts it this way: "We define ourselves by our moods and by our thoughts. We do not just let ourselves be happy or sad . . . we must become a happy person or a sad one" (77).

54. M. Abe, "The Self in Jung and Zen," in Meckel and Moore, eds., *Self and Liberation*, 129.

55. Harré, "The 'Self' as a Theoretical Concept," 404.

56. Charles Taylor, *Sources of the Self*, 35.

57. It might be useful to rename this development the "self complex," to acknowledge the working through of a separate defended state of anxious independence. David Rosen, *Transforming Depression*, (New York: G. P. Putnam's Sons, 1993), 61–84, for a discussion of this.

Chapter 3.
Pandora and the Object of Desire

1. Juliet Mitchell, "Introduction—I," in *Feminine Sexuality: Jacques Lacan and the Ecole Freudienne*, ed. Juliet Mitchell and Jacqueline Rose, trans. Jacqueline Rose (New York: W. W. Norton, 1982), 6.

2. Peter Matthiesen, *Nine-Headed Dragon River* (Boston, Mass.: Shambhala, 1987), 74.

3. For a depiction of the realm of the "Hungry Ghosts" on the Wheel of Life, see Epstein, *Thoughts Without a Thinker*, 28.

4. Alice Miller, *The Drama of the Gifted Child: The Search for the True Self,* trans. R. Ward (New York: Basic Books, 1994).

5. For examples of stage theories of development, see Erik Erikson, *Childhood and Society* (New York: W. W. Norton, 1950); Erikson, *Identity and the Life Cycle;* and C. G. Jung, *Memories, Dreams, Reflections* (New York: Random House, 1961). The importance of chumship for healthy psychological functioning is fully developed in and Harry Stack Sullivan, *The Interpersonal Theory of Psychiatry* (New York: W. W. Norton, 1953).

6. Harold Searles, *Collected Papers on Schizophrenia and Related Subjects* (New York: International Universities Press, 1965), 226–27.

7. The "true self" is the individual's inborn potential for a unique personality, the source of one's authenticity and spontaneity. When there are failures in parenting, the child constructs a secondary personality, a "false self." The false self is a compliant, defensive persona presented to the outside world in order to protect the inner self from psychic annihilation. See D. W. Winnicott, "Ego Distortion in Terms of True and False Self," in *The Maturational Process and the Facilitating Environment,* by D. W. Winnicott, 140–52 (New York: International Universities Press, 1960); D. W. Winnicott, *Human Nature* (New York: Schocken Books, 1988); and D. W. Winnicott, *Playing and Reality* (London: Tavistock, 1971). Many psychotherapists conceive of a true, real, or authentic self and a false self, the latter generally being viewed as resulting from an inadequate parental environment. Jung's early definitions of the "archetype of the self" tend to characterize that archetype as an inborn "supraordinate personality," or pre-existing organization, that is represented by images of the center, the king, the union of opposites, etc. It resembles Winnicott's true self. Psychoanalyst Heinz Kohut also presents and defends the idea of an authentic true self. See Heinz Kohut, *The Analysis of Self* (New York: International Universities Press, 1971).

8. I have discussed the fact that, in our culture, the social context supports the use of appearance as a source of power for women. See Young-Eisendrath and Wiedemann, *Female Authority,* 19–22.

9. Hesiod, *The Works and Days. Theogony. The Shield of Herakles,* trans. R. Lattimore (Ann Arbor: University of Michigan Press, 1959).

10. Ibid., pp. 22–31, lines 54–105.

11. For research that details how female adolescents choose popularity based upon appearance at the expense of achievement, see ch. 2, n. 37, above.

12. Naomi Wolf, *The Beauty Myth: How Images of Beauty Are Used Against Women* (New York: William Morrow, 1991), 12.

13. Epstein, *Thoughts Without a Thinker*, 29.

14. Gregory Bateson, *Steps to an Ecology of Mind* (New York: Ballantine Books, 1972); Gregory Bateson, *Mind and Nature: A Necessary Unity* (New York: Dutton, 1979).

15. Jung, "Psychological Commentary on *The Tibetan Book of the Great Liberation*," 58.

16. The objectification of women in art, literature, and media presentations has been implicated by various researchers in such negative outcomes for women as anorexia nervosa, bulimia, and male violence toward women. See M. Pipher, *Reviving Ophelia: Saving the Selves of Adolescent Girls* (New York: Putnam, 1994); D. G. Linz, E. Donnerstein, and S. Penrod, "Effects of Long-Term Exposure to Violent and Sexually Degrading Depictions of Women," *Journal of Personality and Social Psychology* 55, no. 5 (1988): 758–68; P. A. McLong and D. E. Taub, "Anorexia Nervosa and Bulimia: The Development of Deviant Identities," *Deviant Behavior* 8, no. 2 (1987): 177–89. Also see Mann, *The Difference*, ch. 12; and Wolf, *Beauty Myth*.

17. Wolf, *Beauty Myth*, for discussion on the industry of dieting.

18. Young-Eisendrath, *You're Not What I Expected*, 175.

19. Wolf, *Beauty Myth*, 157.

20. Timothy Beneke, *Men on Rape* (New York: St. Martin's Press, 1982). Rape is rampant today; national studies suggest that 1 in 4 college women claims to have been forced to have sex, and 1 out of 6 is raped. Often this is done by an acquaintance or friend. These statistics are reported in Myra Sadker and David Sadker, *Failing at Fairness*. Also see M. P. Koss, C. A. Gidycz, and N. Wisniewski, "The Scope of Rape: Incidence and Prevalence of Sexual Aggression and Victimization in a National Sample of Higher Education Students," *Journal of Consulting and Clinical Psychology* 55, no. 2 (1987): 162–70. The results of survey interviews suggest that sexual harassment is also very prevalent; see L. Brooks and A. R. Perot, "Reporting Sexual Harassment," *Psychology of Women Quarterly* 15 (1991): 31–47.

  Recent research suggests that among both sexes, but particularly among males, it remains common to justify rape by blaming the victim. Studies have shown that men are more critical of, give more responsibility to, and say more about the characteristics of the rape victim than do women. S. T. Bell, P. J. Kuriloff, and I. Lottes, "Understanding Attributions of Blame in Stranger Rape and Date Rape Situations: An Examination of Gender, Race, Identification, and Students' Social Perceptions of

Rape Victims," *Journal of Applied Social Psychology* 24, no. 19 (1994):
1719–34; G. J. Fischer and J. Chen, "The Attitudes Toward Forcible
Date Rape (FDR) Scale: Development of a Measurement Model," *Journal of Psychopathology and Behavioral Assessment* 16, no. 1 (1994): 33–51;
J. D. Johnson, L. Jackson, L. Gatto, and A. Nowak, "Differential Male
and Female Responses to Inadmissible Sexual History Information Regarding a Rape Victim," *Basic and Applied Social Psychology* 16, no. 4
(1995): 503–13. Even in dating situations, men were more likely than
women to impute sexual meaning to the behaviors of the opposite sex;
see R. M. Kowalski, "Inferring Sexual Interest from Behavioral Cues:
Effects of Gender and Sexually Relevant Attitudes," *Sex Roles* 29 (1993):
13–36.

Rape mentality is already pervasive by the adolescent years. Two
recent surveys of adolescents indicate that females are the target of
sexual harassment more often than males and that its occurrence is
disturbingly common. A. N. LeBlanc, "Harassment in the Hall," *Seventeen*, Sept. 1992, 163–65; Louis Harris and Associates, *Hostile Hallways: The AAUW Survey on Sexual Harassment in America's Schools* (Washington, D.C.: American Association of University Women, 1993). There is
an atmosphere of hostility between the sexes in adolescence, with mild
forms of sexual harassment (snapping bras, unwanted touching, and
comments) going unpunished and ignored by teachers. Even in extreme
cases of harassment and rape, a substantial number of parents respond to
such incidents with the attitude that "boys will be boys."

In spring 1993, a gang of athletes from Lackwood High School in
California was arrested for sex crimes. Apparently, as part of a competition to see who could earn the most points, they had had sex with girls
as young as 10. All but one of the gang members, who claimed that the
girls were willing participants, were released. The district attorney's
office dismissed the incident as a matter for parents, school, and
churches to handle, although sex with a minor is a felony in California.
Judy Mann, in *The Difference*, points out that the Lackwood incident is
just one example of how our culture passively accepts males' violent
behavior, while females are humiliated. She argues that the tendency to
see male violence as inevitable teaches young girls not to challenge
male power.

21. Beneke, *Men on Rape*, 44.
22. Peggy Sanday refers to this as "working a Yes out." Some men treat "no"
as meaningless, because they believe that if they keep trying (even

against physical resistance) or get a girl drunk, she may give in. P. R. Sanday, *Fraternity Gang Rape: Sex, Brotherhood and Privilege on Campus* (New York: New York University Press, 1990).

Chapter 4.
The Subject of Desire

1. Jung discusses intergenerational transmission of neurotic beliefs in C. G. Jung, "The Development of Personality," in Jung, *Collected Works*, vol. 17.

2. For an overview of Jung's concept of transcendent function, see ch. 4, n. 6, below.

3. An exception is "Mental Health: Does Therapy Help?" *Consumer Reports*, Nov. 1995, 734–39. This evaluation revealed that long-term psychotherapy is more effective than short-term therapy.

4. P. Kramer, *Listening to Prozac: A Psychiatrist Explores Anti-Depressant Drugs and the Re-making of the Self.* (New York: Penguin Books, 1994).

5. D. Burns, *Feeling Good.*

6. A. Stevens, *The Two-Million-Year-Old Self* (College Station: Texas A&M University Press, 1993), 117.

7. Ogden, *Matrix of the Mind*, 218.

8. Ibid.

9. Psychoanalyst Thomas Ogden's *Matrix of the Mind* discusses his term "dialogical space," designating the "space" between a symbol (a word or image) and an experience (that which is symbolized). Ogden asks us to recognize that a person always fills that space, that a person is creating a response. The response is not creating the person; we never are merely reactive to our environment or experiences. We always are interactive. Ogden claims that pathologies of the psyche originate mostly in the fantasy that objects are things in themselves, rather than being interpreted by us. Under these circumstances, a hallucination does not *sound* like a voice; it *is* a voice. This kind of objectification of psychological states and emotions is typical both of serious mental illness and of transitory states of shock or confusion. What Ogden alerts us to specifically is the interpreter, the person who "knows" something through her or his own lens or attitude.

The transcendent function, in Jung's words, "is a union of conscious and unconscious contents" that allows a dialectical interplay of different levels or organizations of consciousness. In 1958, Jung wrote a brief commentary for the republication of his 1916 essay, "The Transcendent

Function." In the commentary, he says that this function is "identical with the universal question: How does one come to terms in practice with the unconscious? . . . For the unconscious is not this thing or that; it is the Unknown as it immediately affects us." See C. G. Jung, "The Transcendent Function," in Jung, *Collected Works*, 8:67–68. Here Jung is referring to that which falls outside our capacity to imagine, speak, or fantasize it—the Unknown. Later in the essay, he says that "there is nothing mysterious or metaphysical about the term" (transcendent function). I believe that he is describing the ability to discover something entirely new by holding open the meaning of an event or perception that causes conflict, until one can entertain both (or many) sides of the tension in a new synthesis.

10. G. Dharmasiri, *Buddhist Ethics* (Antioch, Calif.: Golden Leaves Publishing, 1989), 35.

Bibliography

Abe, M. "The Self in Jung and Zen." In *Self and Liberation: The Jung/Buddhism Dialogue*, edited by D. Meckel and R. L. Moore. New York: Paulist Press, 1992.

Adams, G. R., and J. L. Roopnarine. "Physical Attractiveness, Social Skills, and Same-Sex Peer Popularity." *Journal of Group Psychotherapy, Psychodrama, and Sociometry* 47 (1994): 15–35.

Allgood-Merten, B.; P. Lewinsohn; and H. Hops. "Sex Differences and Adolescent Depression." *Journal of Abnormal Psychology* 91, no. 1 (1990): 55–63.

Alm, P. O.; M. Alm; K. Humble; J. Leppert; S. Sorensen; L. Lidberg; and L. Oreland. "Criminality and Platelet Monoamine Oxidase Activity in Former Juvenile Delinquents as Adults." *Acta Psychiatrica Scandinavia* 89 (1994): 41–45.

American Association of University Women. *Shortchanging Girls, Shortchanging America*. Washington, D.C.: Greenberg-Lake, 1991.

Balswick, O. J. *The Inexpressive Male*. Lexington, Mass.: Lexington Books, 1988.

Barnett, Rosalind C., and Grace K. Baruch. *The Competent Woman: Perspectives on Development*. New York: Irvington Publishers, 1978.

Baruch, G., and Barnett, R. "Role Quality, Multiple Role Involvement, and Psychological Well-Being in Midlife Women." *Journal of Personality and Social Psychology* 51 (1986): 578–85.

Bateson, Gregory. *Steps to an Ecology of Mind*. New York: Ballantine Books, 1972.

———. *Mind and Nature: A Necessary Unity*. New York: Dutton, 1979.

Bateson, Mary Catherine. *Peripheral Visions: Learning Along the Way*. New York: Harper Collins, 1994.

Beebe, B., and P. Sloate. "Assessment and Treatment of Difficulties in Mother-Infant Attunement in the First Three Years of Life: A Case History." *Psychoanalytic Inquiry* 1, no. 4 (1982): 601–23.

Beebe, B., and Daniel Stern. "Engagement and Disengagement and Early Object Experiences." In *Communicative Structures and Psychic Structures*, edited by M. Freedman and S. Grand. New York: Plenum Press, 1977.

Bell, S. T.; P. J. Kuriloff; and I. Lottes. "Understanding Attributions of Blame in Stranger Rape and Date Rape Situations: An Examination of Gender, Race, Identification, and Students' Social Perceptions of Rape Victims." *Journal of Applied Social Psychology* 24, no. 19 (1994): 1719–34.

Belsky, J.; L. Steinberg; and P. Drapper. "Childhood Experience, Interpersonal Development, and Reproductive Strategies: An Evolutionary Theory of Socialization." *Child Development* 62 (1991): 647–70.

Beneke, Timothy. *Men on Rape*. New York: St. Martin's Press, 1982.

Blier, M. J., and L. A. Blier-Wilson. "Gender Differences in Self-Rated Emotional Expressiveness." *Sex Roles* 2, nos. 3 and 4 (1989): 287–95.

Broverman, I. K.; S. R. Vogel; D. M. Broverman; F. E. Clarkson; and P. S. Rosenkrantz. "Sex-Role Stereotypes: A Current Appraisal." *Journal of Social Issues* 28 (1972): 59–78.

Brennan, P. A., and S. A. Mednick. "Genetic Perspectives on Crime." *Acta Psychiatrica Scandinavia* 370 (1993): 19–26.

Brooks, L., and A. R. Perot. "Reporting Sexual Harassment." *Psychology of Women Quarterly* 15 (1991): 31–47.

Broverman, I. K.; D. M. Broverman; F. E. Clarkson; P. S. Rosenkrantz; and S. R. Vogel. "Sex-Role Stereotypes and Clinical Judgments of Mental Health." *Journal of Consulting and Clinical Psychology* 34 (1970): 1–7.

Brown, L. M., and Carol Gilligan. *Meeting at the Crossroads: Women's Psychology and Girl's Development*. Cambridge, Mass.: Harvard University Press, 1992.

Bruner, Jerome. *Acts of Meaning*. Cambridge, Mass.: Harvard University Press, 1990.

Children's Defense Fund. *The State of America's Children*. Washington, D.C.: Children's Defense Fund, 1992.

Cole, M., and S. R. Cole. *The Development of Children*. 2d ed. New York: Scientific American Books, 1993.

Coleman, J. *The Adolescent Society*. New York: Free Press, 1961.

Craig, R. S. "The Effect of Television on Gender Portrayals in Television Commercials: A Content Analysis." *Sex Roles* 26 (1992): 197–211.

Crandall, V. J. "Sex Differences in Expectancy of Intellectual and Academic Performance." In *Women: Dependent or Independent Variable?*, edited by Rhoda Unger and F. Denmark, 649–85. New York: Psychological Dimensions, 1975.

Dalai-Lama. *A Policy of Kindness*. Ithaca, N.Y.: Snow Lion Publications, 1990.

Dally, A. *Inventing Motherhood: The Consequences of an Ideal*. New York: Schocken Books, 1982.

Daniels-Beirness, T. "Measuring Peer Status in Boys and Girls: A Problem of Apples and Oranges." In *Social Competence in Developmental Perspective*. 2d ed. Edited by B. H. Schneider, G. Attili, J. Nadel, and R. P. Weissberg. Boston: Kluwer Academic Publishers, 1989.

Derrida, J. "Différance." In *Margins of Philosophy*, by J. Derrida; trans. A. Bass. Chicago: University of Chicago Press, 1982.

―――. *Given Time*. Translated by P. Kamuf. Chicago: University of Chicago Press, 1992.

―――. "How to Avoid Speaking: Denials." In *Derrida and Negation Theology*, edited by K. Frieden. Albany, N.Y.: SUNY Press, 1974.

―――. *Positions*. Translated by A. Bass. Chicago: University of Chicago Press, 1981.

―――. *The Post Card: From Socrates to Freud and Beyond*. Translated by A. Bass. Chicago: University of Chicago Press, 1987.

Dharmasiri, G. *Buddhist Ethics*. Antioch, Calif.: Golden Leaves Publishing, 1989.

Douglas, Claire. *The Woman in the Mirror: Analytic Psychology and the Feminine*. Boston: Sigo Press, 1990.

Dweck, C., et al. "Sex Differences in Learned Helplessness: II. The Contingencies of Evaluative Feedback in the Classroom; and III. An Experimental Analysis." *Developmental Psychology* 14 (1978): 268–76.

Eaton, W. W., and L. G. Kessler. *Epidemiologic Field Methods in Psychiatry: The NIMH Epidemiologic Catchment Area Program*. Orlando, Fla.: Academic Press, 1985.

Ehrhardt, A. A., and H. F. L. Meyer-Bahlburg. "Effects of Prenatal Sex Hormones on Gender-Related Behavior." *Science* 211 (1981): 1312–18.

Eisenberg, Nancy, and R. Lennon. "Sex Differences in Empathy and Related Capacities." *Psychological Bulletin* 94 (1983): 100–31.

Epstein, M. *Thoughts Without a Thinker: Psychotherapy from a Buddhist Perspective*. New York: Basic Books, 1995.

Erikson, Erik. *Childhood and Society*. New York: W. W. Norton, 1950.

―――. *Identity and the Life Cycle*. New York: W. W. Norton, 1980.

Fagot, B. I., and R. Hagan. "Observations of Parent Reactions to Sex-Stereotyped Behaviors: Age and Sex Effects." *Child Development* 62, no. 3 (1991): 617–28.

Fairbairn, W. R. D. *An Object-Relations Theory of the Personality*. New York: Basic Books, 1952.

Faludi, S. *Backlash: The Undeclared War Against American Women*. New York: Crown, 1991.

Farver, J., and S. Wimbarti. "Paternal Participation in Toddlers' Pretend Play." *Social Development* 4, no. 1 (1995): 17–31.

Feiring, C., and M. Lewis. "The Child's Social Network: Sex Differences from Three to Six Years." *Sex Roles* 17 (1987): 621–36.

Fennema, E., and L. Leder. *Mathematics and Gender*. New York: Teachers College Press, Columbia University, 1990.

Fischer, G. J., and J. Chen. "The Attitudes Toward Forcible Date Rape (FDR) Scale: Development of a Measurement Model." *Journal of Psychopathology and Behavioral Assessment* 16, no. 1 (1994): 33–51.

Fisher, T. D. "Adult Toy Purchases for Children: Factors Affecting Sex-Typed Toy Selection." *Journal of Applied Developmental Psychology* 14, no. 3 (1993): 385–406.

Flax, Jane. *Disputed Subjects: Essays on Psychoanalysis, Politics, and Philosophy*. New York: Routledge, 1993.

———. "Post-Modernism and Gender Relations in Feminist Theory." *Signs* 12, no. 4 (1987): 621–43.

———. "Remembering the Selves: Is the Repressed Gendered?" *Michigan Quarterly Review* 26, no. 1 (1986): 92–110.

———. *Thinking Fragments: Psychoanalysis, Feminism, and Postmodernism in the Contemporary West*. Berkeley, Calif.: University of California Press, 1990.

Freud, Sigmund. "Some Psychical Consequences of the Anatomical Distinction Between the Sexes." In *Standard Edition of the Complete Works of Sigmund Freud*, edited by J. Strachey. Volume 19. 1925; reprinted London: Hogarth Press, 1961.

Furnham, A., and R. Rawles. "Sex Differences in the Estimation of Intelligence." *Journal of Social Behavior and Personality* 10, no. 3 (1995): 741–48.

Gadamer, H. G. *Philosophical Hermeneutics*. Berkeley, Calif.: University of California Press, 1977.

———. *Truth and Method*. New York: Crossroads, 1982.

Gilligan, Carol. "The Centrality of Relationship in Human Development." Paper presented at the Symposium of the Jean Piaget Society, Montreal, Quebec, Canada, May 1992.

———. *In a Different Voice: Psychological Theory and Women's Development*. Cambridge, Mass.: Harvard University Press, 1982.

———. "Woman's Place in Man's Life Cycle." *Harvard Educational Review* 49, no. 4 (1979): 431–46.

———. "Women's Psychological Development: Implications for Psychotherapy." In *Women, Girls, and Psychotherapy: Reframing Resistance*, edited by Carol Gilligan, G. Rogers, and D. L. Tolman, 5–31. Binghamton, N.Y.: Harrington Park Press, 1991.

Goldstein, J., and J. Kornfield. *Seeking the Heart of Wisdom: The Path of Insight Meditation.* Boston: Shambhala, 1987.

Goleman, D. *Emotional Intelligence.* New York: Bantam Books, 1995.

Hamid, N., and D. Lok. "Gender Stereotyping in Estimates of Intelligence in Chinese Students." *Journal of Social Psychology* 135, no. 3 (1995): 407–409.

Harding, Sandra. *Whose Science, Whose Knowledge: Thinking from Women's Lives.* Ithaca, N.Y.: Cornell University Press, 1991.

Harré, Rom. *Personal Being: A Theory for Individual Psychology.* Oxford, England: Basil Blackwell, 1983.

———. "The 'Self' as a Theoretical Concept." In *Relativism: Interpretation and Confrontation*, edited by M. Krausz. Notre Dame, Ind.: University of Notre Dame Press, 1989.

———. *Social Being.* Cambridge, Mass.: Blackwell, 1979.

Hazzard, W. R. "Biological Basis of the Sex Differential in Longevity." *Journal of the American Geriatrics Society* 34, no. 6 (1986): 455–71.

Heidegger, M. *Basic Concepts: 1889–1976.* Translated by G. E. Aylesworth. Bloomington, Ind.: University of Indiana Press, 1993.

———. *The Basic Problems of Phenomenology: 1889–1976.* Translated by A. Hofstadter. Bloomington, Ind.: Indiana University Press, 1982.

———. *Being and Time.* New York: Harper and Row, 1962.

Heilbrun, Carolyn G. *Hamlet's Mother and Other Women.* New York: Columbia University Press, 1990.

Herman, B. "Changing Sources of Self-Esteem among Boys and Girls in Secondary Schools." *Urban Education* 24 (1990): 432–39.

Hesiod. *The Works and Days. Theogony. The Shield of Herakles.* Translated by Richmond Lattimore. Ann Arbor: University of Michigan Press, 1959.

Intons-Peterson, M. J., and Reddel, M. "What Do People Ask about a Neonate?" *Developmental Psychology* 20 (1984): 358–59.

Izard, C. E. "Basic Emotions, Relations among Emotions, and Emotion-Cognition Relations." *Psychological Review* 99, no. 3 (1992): 561–65.

———. "Emotions as Motivations: An Evolutionary-Developmental Perspective." *Nebraska Symposium on Motivation* 26 (1978): 163–200.

———. *Human Emotions.* New York: Plenum Press, 1977.

———. "Innate and Universal Facial Expressions: Evidence from Developmental and Cross-Cultural Research." *Psychological Bulletin* 115, no. 2 (1994): 288–99.

Jack, Dana. "Silencing the Self: The Power of Social Imperatives in Female Depression." In *Depression and Women: A Lifespan Perspective*, edited by R. Formanek and A. Gurian. New York: Springer Publishing Company, 1987.

Jacklin, C. N.; J. A. DiPietro; and E. E. Maccoby. "Sex-Typing Behavior and Sex-Typing Pressure in Child-Parent Interaction." *Archives of Sexual Behavior* 13, no. 5 (1985): 413–25.

Jacklin, C. N., and E. E. Maccoby. "Social Behavior at Thirty-Three Months in Same-Sex and Mixed-Sex Dyads." *Child Development* 49, no. 3 (1978): 557–69.

Johnson, J. D.; L. Jackson; L. Gatto; and A. Nowak. "Differential Male and Female Responses to Inadmissible Sexual History Information Regarding a Rape Victim." *Basic and Applied Social Psychology* 16, no. 4 (1995): 503–13.

Jordan, J. V.; A. Kaplan; J. B. Miller; I. Stiver; and J. Surrey. *Women's Growth in Connection: Writings from the Stone Center*. New York: Guilford Press, 1991.

Jung, C. G. *The Collected Works of C. G. Jung*, 2d ed. Translated by R. F. C. Hull. 9:11–22. Princeton, N.J.: Princeton University Press, 1959.

———. *Letters*. vol. I. Princeton, N.J.: Princeton University Press, 1973.

———. *Memories, Dreams, Reflections*. Edited by A. Jaffâe. New York: Pantheon, 1963.

Kapleau, Philip. *The Three Pillars of Zen*. New York: Doubleday, 1965.

Kast, Verena. *The Nature of Loving: Patterns of Human Relationship*. Translated by B. Matthews. Wilmette, Ill.: Chiron Publications, 1986.

Klein, Ann. *Meeting the Great Bliss Queen: Buddhists, Feminists, and the Art of the Self*. Boston: Beacon Press, 1994.

Klein, Melanie. *Envy and Gratitude and Other Works*. New York: Free Press, 1975.

Kline, B. E., and E. B. Short. "Changes in Emotional Resilience: Gifted Adolescent Females." *Roeper Review* 13, no. 3 (1991): 118–21.

Kohlberg, Lawrence. "A Cognitive Developmental Analysis of Children's Sex-Role Concepts and Attitudes." In *The Development of Sex Differences*, edited by E. E. Maccoby. Stanford, Calif.: Stanford University Press, 1966.

Kohut, H. *The Analysis of Self*. New York: International Universities Press, 1971.

Komarovsky, M. *Dilemmas of Masculinity: A Study of College Youth*. New York: W. W. Norton, 1976.

Kornfield, J. *A Path With Heart: A Guide Through the Perils and Promises of Spiritual Life*. New York: Bantam Books, 1993.

Koss, M. P.; C. A. Gidycz; and N. Wisniewski. "The Scope of Rape: Incidence and Prevalence of Sexual Aggression and Victimization in a National Sample of Higher Education Students." *Journal of Consulting and Clinical Psychology* 55, no. 2 (1987): 162–70.

Kowalski, R. M. "Inferring Sexual Interest from Behavioral Cues: Effects, Gender and Sexually Relevant Attitudes." *Sex Roles* 29 (1993): 13–36.

Kramer, L. "Gifted Adolescent Girls: Self-Perceptions of Ability within One Middle School Setting." Ph.D. diss., University of Florida, 1985.

Krupnick, C. "Unlearning Gender Roles." In *Gender and Public Policy: Cases and Comments,* edited by K. Winston and M. Bane. Boulder, Colo.: Westview Press, 1992.

LeBlanc, A. N. "Harassment in the Hall." *Seventeen,* September, 1992, 163–65.

Leinhardt, G., A. Seewald, and M. Engel. "Learning What's Taught: Sex Differences in Instruction." *Journal of Educational Psychology* 71 (1979) 432–39.

Lerner, Harriet Goldhor. "Female Depression: Self-Sacrifice and Self-Betrayal in Relationships." In *Depression and Women: A Lifespan Perspective,* edited by R. Formanek and A. Gurian. New York: Springer Publishing Company, 1987.

Lester, D. *Why People Kill Themselves: A 1990s Summary of Research Findings on Suicide Behavior.* Springfield, Ill.: Charles C. Thompson, 1992.

Lewinsohn, P. M., et al. "Adolescent Psychopathology: II. Psychosocial Risk Factors for Depression." *Journal of Abnormal Psychology* 103, no. 2 (1994): 302–15.

Lewis, M. "Self-Conscious Emotions and the Development of Self." *Journal of the American Psychoanalytic Association* 39, Suppl. (1991): 45–73.

Lewis, M., and L. A. Rosenblum. *The Development of Affect.* New York: Plenum Press, 1978.

Lichtenberg, J. D. "Implications for Psychoanalytic Theory of Research on the Neonate." *International Review of Psycho-Analysis* 8, no. 1 (1981): 35–52.

———. "Mirrors and Mirroring: Developmental Experiences." *Psychoanalytic Inquiry* 5, no. 2 (1985): 199–210.

———. *Psychoanalysis and Infant Research.* Hillsdale, N.J.: Analytic Press, 1983.

Lichtenberg, J. D., and D. G. Norton. *Cognitive and Mental Development in the First Five Years of Life: A Review of Recent Research.* Chevy Chase, Md.: National Institute of Mental Health, 1970.

Linz, D. G.; E. Donnerstein; and S. Penrod. "Effects of Long-Term Exposure to Violent and Sexually Degrading Depictions of Women." *Journal of Personality and Social Psychology* 55, no. 5 (1988): 758–68.

Loevinger, Jane. *Ego Development.* San Francisco, Calif.: Jossey-Bass, 1976.

Louis Harris and Associates. *Hostile Hallways: The AAUW Survey on Sexual Harassment in America's Schools*. Washington, D.C.: American Association of University Women, 1993.

Maccoby, E. E. "Gender and Relationships: A Developmental Account." *American Psychologist* 45, no. 4 (1990): 513–20.

———. "Gender and Relationships: A Reprise." *American Psychologist* 46, no. 5 (1991): 538–39.

———. "Gender as a Social Category." *Developmental Psychology* 24, no. 6 (1988): 755–65.

MacDonald, K., and R. Parke. "Parent-Child Physical Play: The Effects of Sex and Age of Children and Parents." *Sex Roles* 15 (1986): 367–78.

MacDonald, K. B. *Social and Personality Development: An Evolutionary Synthesis*. New York: Plenum Press, 1988.

McLong, P. A., and D. E. Taub. "Anorexia Nervosa and Bulimia: The Development of Deviant Identities." *Deviant Behavior* 8, no. 2 (1987): 177–89.

MacLusky, N. J., and F. Naftolin. "Sexual Differentiation of the Central Nervous System." *Science* 211 (1981): 1294–1303.

MacMurray, John. *The Form of the Personal*. 2 Volumes. London: Faber and Faber, 1957 and 1961.

McNeely, Deldon. *Women and the Trickster*. Woodstock, Conn.: Spring Publications, 1996.

Mann, Judy. *The Difference: Growing Up Female in America*. New York: Warner Books, 1994.

Martin, C. L.; L. Eisenbud; and H. Rose. "Children's Gender-Based Reasoning about Toys." *Child Development* 66, no. 5 (1995): 1453–72.

Matthiesen, P. *Nine-Headed Dragon River*. Boston: Shambhala, 1987.

Mattoon, Mary Ann, and Jennifer Jones. "Is the Animus Obsolete?" *Quadrant* 20, no. 1 (1987): 5–22.

Meckel, D. J., and R. L. Moore, eds. *Self and Liberation: The Jung/Buddhism Dialogue*. Mahwah, N.Y.: Paulist Press, 1992.

Mediamark Research Multimedia Audience Report, Spring 1990. New York: Mediamark Research, Inc., 1990.

"Mental Health: Does Therapy Help?" *Consumer Reports*, November, 1995, 734–39.

Miller, Alice. *The Drama of the Gifted Child: The Search for the True Self*. Translated by R. Ward. New York: Basic Books, 1994.

Mirowsky, J., and C. E. Ross. "Sex Differences in Distress: Real or Artifact?" *American Sociological Review* 60, no. 3 (1995): 449–68.

Mitchell, Juliet, and Jacqueline Rose, eds. *Feminine Sexuality: Jacques Lacan and the Ecole Freudienne*. Translated by Jacqueline Rose. New York: W. W. Norton, 1982.

Mitchell, S. *Hope and Dread in Psychoanalysis*. New York: Basic Books, 1993.

———. *Relational Concepts in Psychoanalysis: An Integration*. Cambridge, Mass.: Harvard University Press, 1984.

Money, John. "Differentiation of Gender Identity." *JSAS Catalog of Selected Documents in Psychology* 6, no. 4 (1976).

Money, John, and A. A. Ehrhardt. *Man and Woman, Boy and Girl: The Differentiation and Dimorphism of Gender Identity from Conception to Maturity*. Baltimore, Md.: Johns Hopkins University Press, 1972.

Moran, P. B., and J. Eckenrode. "Gender Differences in the Costs and Benefits of Peer Relationships during Adolescence." *Journal of Adolescent Research* 6, no. 4 (1991): 396–409.

Nolen-Hoeksema, S. "Sex Differences in Unipolar Depression: Evidence and Theory." *Psychological Bulletin* 101, no. 2 (1987): 259–82.

Nolen-Hoeksema, S., and J. S. Girgus. "The Emergence of Gender Differences in Depression during Adolescence." *Psychological Bulletin* 115, no. 3 (1994): 424–43.

Ogden, Thomas H. *The Matrix of the Mind: Object Relations and the Psychoanalytic Dialogue*. Northvale, N.J.: Jason Aronson, 1986.

Overton, W. F. "The Arrow of Time and the Cycle of Time: Concepts of Change, Cognition, and Embodiment." *Psychological Inquiry* 5, no. 3 (1994): 215–37.

———. "Historical and Contemporary Perspectives on Developmental Theory and Research Strategies." *Visions of Aesthetics, the Environment, and Development: The Legacy of Joachim Wohlwill*. Edited by R. Downs, L. Liben and D. Palermo. Hillsdale, N.J.: Lawrence Erlbaum, 1991.

———. "The Structure of Developmental Theory." *Advances in Child Development and Behavior*. Edited by H. W. Reese. New York: Academic Press, 1991.

———. "Contexts of Meaning: The Computational and Embodied Mind." In *The Nature and Ontogenesis of Meaning*, edited by W. F. Overton and D. S. Palermo, 1–18. Hillsdale, N.J.: Lawrence Erlbaum, 1994.

———. "Historical and Contemporary Perspectives on Developmental Theory and Research Strategies." In *Visions of Aesthetics, the Environment, and Development: The Legacy of Joachim Wohlwill*, edited by R. Downs, L. Liben, and D. Palermo, 263–311. Hillsdale, N.J.: Lawrence Erlbaum, 1991.

———. "Metaphor, Recursive Systems, and Paradox in Science and Developmental Theory." In *Advances in Child Development and Behavior*, edited by H. W. Reese, 23:59–71. New York: Academic Press, 1991.

————. "The Structure of Developmental Theory." In *Advances in Child Development and Behavior*, edited by H. W. Reese, 23:1–37. New York: Academic Press, 1991.

————. "World Views and Their Influence on Psychological Theory and Research: Kuhn-Lakatos-Laudan." In *Advances in Child Development and Behavior*, edited by H. W. Reese, 18:191–226. New York: Academic Press, 1984.

Pellett, T. L., and J. M. Harrison. "Children's Perceptions of the Gender Appropriateness of Physical Activities: A Further Analysis." *Play and Culture* 5, no. 3 (1992): 305–13.

Petersen, Anne C. "The Gangly Years." *Psychology Today*, September, 1987, pp. 28–34.

Petersen, Anne C.; P. A. Sarigiani; and R. E. Kennedy. "Adolescent Depression: Why More Girls?" *Journal of Youth and Adolescence* 20, no. 2 (1991): 247–71.

Piaget, J. *The Origins of Intelligence in Children*. New York: International Universities Press, 1952.

————. *Six Psychological Studies*. New York: Random House, 1967.

Pipher, Mary. *Reviving Ophelia: Saving the Selves of Adolescent Girls*. New York: Putnam, 1994.

Pleck, J., and R. Brannon. "Male Roles and the Male Experience." *Journal of Social Issues* 34 (1978): 1–4.

Quine, W. V. *Philosophy of Logic*. 2d ed. Cambridge, Mass.: Harvard University Press, 1986.

————. *The Philosophy of W. V. Quine*. Edited by L. E. Hahn and P. A. Schilpp. La Salle, Ill.: Open Court, 1986.

————. *Pursuit of Truth*. Cambridge, Mass.: Harvard University Press, 1990.

Rahula, W. *What the Buddha Taught*. New York: Grove Press, 1959.

Rich, Adrienne. *Of Woman Born: Motherhood as Experience and Institution*. New York: W. W. Norton, 1976.

Roggman, L. A., and J. C. Peery. "Parent-Infant Social Play in Brief Encounters: Early Gender Differences." *Child Study Journal* 19, no. 1 (1989): 65–79.

Rorty, R. *The Consequences of Pragmatism*. Princeton, N.J.: Princeton University Press, 1982.

————. *Contingency, Irony, and Solidarity*. Cambridge, England: Cambridge University Press, 1989.

————. "Inquiry as Recontextualization: An Anti-Dualist Account of Interpretation." In *The Interpretive Turn: Philosophy, Science, Culture*, edited by D. R. Hiley, J. F. Bohman, and R. Shusterman, 59–80. Ithaca, N.Y.: Cornell University Press, 1991.

Rosen, David. *The Tao of Jung: The Way of Integrity*. New York: Viking, 1996.

———. *Transforming Depression*. New York: G. P. Putnam's Sons, 1993.

Roseneau, P. M. *Postmodernism and the Social Sciences: Insights, Inroads, and Intrusions*. Princeton, N.J.: Princeton University Press, 1992.

Rubin, J. Z.; F. J. Provenzano; and Z. Luria. "The Eye of the Beholder: Parents' Views on Sex of Newborns." *American Journal of Orthopsychiatry* 43 (1974): 720–31.

Ruble, D. "Sex-Role Development." In *Development Psychology: An Advanced Textbook*, edited by M. H. Bornstein and M. E. Lamb. Hillsdale, N.J.: Lawrence Erlbaum, 1983.

Russo, N. F. "Forging Research Priorities for Women's Mental Health." *American Psychologist* 45, no. 3 (1990): 368–73.

Sadker, Myra, and Sadker, David. *Failing at Fairness: How America's Schools Cheat Girls*. New York: Macmillan, 1994.

———. "Sexism in the Classroom: From Grade School to Graduate School." *Phi Delta Kappan* 67 (1986): 512–15.

———. *Year 3: Final Report: Promoting Effectiveness in Classroom Instruction*. Washington, D.C.: National Institute for Education, 1984.

Samuels, Andrew. *The Plural Psyche: Personality, Morality, and the Father*. London: Routledge, 1989.

Sanday, P. R. *Female Power and Male Dominance: On the Origins of Sexual Inequality*. Cambridge, England: Cambridge University Press, 1981.

———. *Fraternity Gang Rape: Sex, Brotherhood, and Privilege on Campus*. New York: New York University Press, 1990.

Sandler, B., and R. Hall. *The Classroom Climate: A Chilly One for Women*. Washington, D.C.: Association of American Colleges, 1982.

Schafer, Roy. *Language and Insight*. New Haven, Conn.: Yale University Press, 1978.

———. *A New Language for Psychoanalysis*. New Haven, Conn.: Yale University Press, 1976.

———. *Retelling a Life: Narration and Dialogue in Psychoanalysis*. New York: Basic Books, 1992.

Searles, H. *Collected Papers on Schizophrenia and Related Subjects*. New York: International Universities Press, 1965.

Seavey, C. A.; P. A. Katz; and S. R. Zalk. "Baby X: The Effect of Gender Labels on Adult Responses to Infant." *Sex Roles* 1 (1975): 103–10.

Seidenberg, R. "Psychoanalysis and Femininity." Part 2. *Psychoanalytic Psychology* 8, no. 2 (1991): 225–37.

Singer, J. *Androgyny: Toward a New Theory of Sexuality*. New York: Anchor Books, 1977.

Snow, M. E.; C. N. Jacklin; and E. E. Maccoby. "Sex-of-Child Differences in Father-Child Interaction at One Year of Age." *Child Development* 54, no. 1 (1983): 227–32.

Spence, D. *The Freudian Metaphor: Toward Paradigm Change in Psychoanalysis.* New York: W. W. Norton, 1987.

———. *Narrative Truth, Historical Truth.* New York: W. W. Norton, 1982.

Stern, Daniel N. "Affect Attunement." In *Frontiers of Infant Psychiatry,* edited by J. D. Call; E. Galenson; and R. L. Tyson. Volume 2. New York: Basic Books, 1985.

———. *The Interpersonal World of the Infant.* New York: Basic Books, 1985.

Stevens, A. *The Two-Million-Year-Old Self.* College Station: Texas A&M University Press, 1993.

Stipek, D. J. "Sex Differences in Children's Attributions for Success and Failure on Math and Spelling Tests." *Sex Roles* 11 (1984): 969–81.

Strawson, P. F. *Individuals: An Essay in Descriptive Metaphysics.* London: Methuen, 1959.

Sullivan, H. S. *The Interpersonal Theory of Psychiatry.* New York: W. W. Norton, 1953.

Suzuki, S. *Zen Mind, Beginner's Mind.* Edited by T. Dixon. New York: Weatherhill, 1970.

Tannen, D. *You Just Don't Understand: Women and Men in Conversation.* New York: William Morrow, 1990.

Tavris, Carol. *The Mismeasure of Woman.* New York: Simon and Schuster, 1992.

Taylor, Charles. "The Dialogical Self." In *The Interpretive Turn: Philosophy, Science, Culture,* edited by D. R. Hiley, J. F. Bohman, and R. Shusterman. Ithaca, N.Y.: Cornell University Press, 1991.

———. *The Ethics of Authenticity.* Cambridge, Mass.: Harvard University Press, 1992.

———. *Human Agency and Language: Philosophical Papers.* Volume 1. Cambridge, England: Cambridge University Press, 1985.

———. *Philosophical Arguments.* Cambridge, Mass.: Harvard University Press, 1995.

———. *Sources of the Self: The Making of the Modern Identity.* Cambridge, Mass.: Harvard University Press, 1989.

Tompkins, S. S. *Affect, Imagery, and Consciousness.* Volume 1: *The Positive Affects.* New York: Springer, 1962.

———. *Affect, Imagery, and Consciousness.* Volume 2: *The Negative Affects.* New York: Springer, 1963.

Trautner, H. "Boys' and Girls' Play Behavior in Same-Sex and Opposite-Sex Pairs." *Journal of Genetic Psychology* 156 (1995): 5–15.

Trivers, R. "Parent-Offspring Conflict." *American Zoologist* 14 (1974): 249–64

Unger, Rhoda. *Representations: Social Constructions of Gender.* Los Gatos, Calif.: Baywood Publishers, 1989.

Vande Berg, L. R., and D. Streckfuss. "Prime-Time Television's Portrayal of Women and the World of Work: A Demographic Profile." *Journal of Broadcasting and Electronic Media* 36, no. 2 (1992): 195–208.

Verbrugge, L. M. "Gender and Health: An Update on Hypotheses and Evidence." *Journal of Health and Social Behavior* 26, no. 3 (1985): 156–82.

Wagman, B., and N. Folbre. "The Feminization of Inequality: Some New Patterns." *Challenge* 31, no. 6 (1988): 56–59.

Watts, W. D., and L. S. Wright. "The Relationship of Alcohol, Tobacco, Marijuana, and Other Illegal Drug Use to Delinquency among Mexican-American, Black, and White Adolescent Males." *Adolescence* 25 (1990): 171–81.

Wehr, Demaris S. *Jung and Feminism: Liberating Archetypes.* Boston: Beacon Press, 1987.

Weinraub, M.; L. P. Clemens; A. Sockloff; T. Ethridge; E. Gracely; and B. Myers. "The Development of Sex-Role Stereotypes in the Third Year: Relationships to Gender Labeling, Gender Identity, Sex-Typed Toy Preference, and Family Characteristics." *Child Development* 55 (1984): 1493–1503.

Weissman, M. M., and G. L. Klerman. "Sex Differences and the Epidemiology of Depression." *Archives of General Psychiatry* 34 (1977): 98–111.

Werner, Heinz. "The Concept of Development from a Comparative and Organismic Point of View." In *The Concept of Development: An Issue in the Study of Human Behavior.* Edited by D. B. Harris, 125–48. Minneapolis: University of Minnesota Press, 1957.

Wilkinson, L. C., and C. Marrett, eds. *Gender Influences in Classroom Interaction.* Orlando, Fla.: Academic Press, 1985.

Winnicott, D. W. "Ego Distortion in Terms of True and False Self." In *The Maturational Process and the Facilitating Environment,* by D. W. Winnicott, 140–52. New York: International Universities Press, 1960.

———. *Human Nature.* New York: Schocken Books, 1988.

———. *Playing and Reality.* London: Tavistock, 1971.

Wittgenstein, L. *Philosophical Investigations.* Oxford, England: Blackwell, 1968.

———. *Philosophical Occasions: 1912–1951.* Edited by J. C. Klagge and A. Nordmann. Indianapolis, Ind.: Hacket Publishing Company, 1993.

————. *The Wittgenstein Reader: 1889–1951*. Edited by A. Kenny. Cambridge, Mass.: Blackwell, 1994.

Wolf, Naomi. *The Beauty Myth: How Images of Beauty Are Used Against Women.* New York: William Morrow, 1991.

Woolf, Virginia. *A Room of One's Own.* Middlesex, England: Penguin Books, 1928.

Yee, D. K., and J. S. Eccles. "Parent Perceptions and Attributions for Children's Math Achievement." *Sex Roles* 19 (1988): 317–33.

Young-Eisendrath, Polly. "Gender and Individuation: Relating to Self and Other." In *Mirrors of Transformation: The Self in Relationships*, edited by D. E. Brien, 21–39. Berwyn, Penn.: Round Table Press, 1995.

————. "Gender, Animus, and Related Topics." In *Gender and Soul in Psychotherapy*, edited by Nathan Schwart-Salant and M. Stein. Wilmette, Ill.: Chiron, 1991.

————. *The Gifts of Suffering: Finding Insight, Compassion, and Renewal.* Reading, Mass.: Addison-Wesley, 1996.

————. *Hags and Heroes: A Feminist Approach to Jungian Psychotherapy with Couples.* Toronto, Canada: Inner City Books, 1984.

————. "Rethinking Feminism, the Animus, and the Feminine." In *To Be a Woman*, edited by C. Zweig. Los Angeles, Calif.: Tarcher, 1990.

————. *You're Not What I Expected: Learning to Love the Opposite Sex.* New York: William Morrow, 1993.

Young-Eisendrath, Polly, and James A. Hall. *Jung's Self Psychology: A Constructivist Perspective.* New York: Guilford Press, 1991.

————. "Ways of Speaking of Self." In *The Book of the Self: Person, Pretext, and Process*, edited by Polly Young-Eisendrath and James A. Hall. New York: New York University Press, 1987.

Young-Eisendrath, Polly, and Florence L. Wiedemann. *Female Authority: Empowering Women through Psychotherapy.* New York: Guilford Press, 1987.

Index

Abe, Masao, 55–56

achievement estimation, 46–49, 104–107n 34–37

adolescent development: achievement estimation, 46–48, 104–107n 34–37; and objectification of females, 62–63, 66, 71, 73; strange gender, 39

adult development: appeal to universals, 18–19; and gender identity, 40; and mid-life crises, 48–49, 68, 108–109n 40; multiplicity of self, 57; self as subject of desire, 70–71, 79–90; of self-reflection, 50–51, 57

affirmative postmodernism, 16–17, 23, 96n 18

agency, restoration of, 70–71. See also subject of desire, self as

aggressiveness, reproductive reward for, 67

analytical psychology: contrasexuality contribution, 46; essentialism in, 13–15, 17, 30–33, 101n 14; flexibility of gender identity, 35; and postmodernism, 8–17, 21, 23, 96n 18; realist critique of, 83–84; and Zen Buddhism, 53–54. See also psychotherapy

anima and animus theory, 42–44. See also contrasexuality; Other, subjective

archetype: and complexes, 19–24, 97n 22; and constraints on human psychology, 17–19; and contrasexuality, 32–33, 37, 43; embodiment as, 16–17; and emotion, 14–15, 26, 97n 22; universality of, 10–11, 13, 25, 31. See also Self, archetype of

Atman, 54

autonomy, gender valuation of, 29, 63

Bateson, Gregory, 69

Bateson, Mary Catherine, 29

beauty myth. See female beauty myth

beliefs, and concept of self, 52

Beneke, Tim, 74–75

biology: vs. embodiment, 16–17; non-essentialist nature of, 25–26; as sole source for mental experience, 4. See also essentialism, biological; realism, modern scientific